Cut-Loose Quilts
Stack, Slice, Switch, *and* Sew

Jan Mullen

C&T PUBLISHING

Copyright © 2001 by Jan Mullen

Development Editor: Cyndy Lyle Rymer

Technical Editors: Sara Kate MacFarland, Karyn Hoyt, Peggy Kass, Joyce Engels Lytle, and Lynn Koolish

Book Design and Design Direction: Kristen Yenche

Cover Design and Production: Kristen Yenche

Production Assistant: Kirstie L. McCormick

Production Coordination: Diane Pedersen

Graphic Illustrations: Richard Sheppard

Cover Image: *Beggar Block Butterfliez #2–Springtime* by Jan Mullen, 42³⁄₄" x 52³⁄₄", 2000.

Photography by Bewley Shaylor

Attention Teachers:

C&T Publishing, Inc. encourages you to use this book as a text for teaching. Contact us at 800-284-1114 or www.ctpub.com for more information about the C&T Teachers Program.

Library of Congress Cataloging-in-Publication Data

Mullen, Jan
  Cut-loose quilts : stack, slice, switch, and sew / Jan Mullen.
    p. cm.
Includes index.
  ISBN 1-57120-154-8
  1. Patchwork--Patterns. 2. Machine quilting. 3. Patchwork quilts.
  I. Title.
  TT835 .M823 2001
  746.46'041--dc21

                                        00-011628

Published by C&T Publishing, Inc.
P.O. Box 1456
Lafayette, California 94549

Printed in Hong Kong

10 9 8 7 6 5 4 3 2 1

Dedication

This book is dedicated to my aunt, the late Bonnie Hurry, a role model and mentor when I was choosing to take the creative road.

Acknowledgments

With thanks to Ben, Brodie, Keelan, and Miffany, who have gone without home-cooked bikkies, ironed clothes, and my presence so I could pursue my crooked path.

My twin in black, Bewley Shaylor, for the laughs and the photography.

All at C&T for making it so easy; in particular, Cyndy Rymer, owner of the red pen.

Ben, again, for lighter use of the red pen, and Miffy, for pinning most of these quilts.

My student guinea pigs, Marilyn Dillon, Jan Holland, Julie Howell, Tess Marks, Marilyn Matich, Debra J. McHolick, Jan Morgan, and Gail Samuel for their enthusiasm, perseverance, and constructive criticism. And for advice and encouragement in establishing a higher profile for Stargazey Quilts: Vince Parry and Allan Murphy of XLN Fabrics, Bonnie Benson and Mike Koen of Quilters' Resource, and Faye Burgos and Stephanie Dell'Olio of Marcus Brothers Fabrics.

CONTENTS

First Crooked Steps

Sometimes it takes just a moment of creative thought to change direction. The bright light gets turned on, and you have the experience that changes the way you look at things. Let me tell you what happened to me when I decided to go out on my own and start my business, Stargazey Quilts...

A few members of the sewing group in which I was involved decided to organize a round robin quilt. We started with a center block each, and then in turn had to add a border on the other five tops as they came to us. My friend Jane's quilt, on page 7, had an appliquéd block of hovering angels. When her quilt came to me, I thought the angels really needed to be looking back down to earth—at a border of houses! Problem: these houses needed to be small and numerous to fit within a border setting and they also needed to be quirky. Inspiration! I quickly sketched a variety of simple crooked houses that could be machine-pieced easily and would suit the primitive look of the angels. In no time I had a quick sketch of houses, cups, flying goosez, Log Cabins, teapots, and so on, following the same lines of thought. This was the true birth of Stargazey Quilts, which has kept me focused on designing and making crooked blocks ever since.

The quest for turning both pictoral and traditional blocks into crooked versions has been moderated by my desire as a teacher to make these versions easily repeatable and accessible to all skill levels. I had to devise techniques of making crooked blocks with easy methods. I had to break rules and make others comfortable following suit. This book is a compilation of some of these basic methods—all easy to cut and sew. The techniques are accessible to beginners, yet challenging enough to inspire the more experienced to modify their favorite blocks or to make up new ones of their own.

This book is based solely on geometric traditional blocks, but it is not a definitive book. I don't include all of the traditional blocks that could be used this way. I give you blocks that derive from the most commonly used patchwork units, and, just as importantly, blocks whose look I like. I give you starting points, techniques, ideas, and hopefully, inspiration. I work from a few basic guiding principles and "proper" math is not necessarily well heeded or needed! My aim is to introduce you to the idea of making the insides of the blocks crooked, individual, unique, and to give you the ability to do so.

Everyone will produce work of a slightly different style. People who are precise and organized will produce work that reflects their personality. Other people are more spontaneous and may like to push boundaries to create work that may lose points and gain flair! You can go your own way, follow your own crooked path.

Editor's Note: With respect to Jan's wicked wayz, we have honored her use of the letter z at the end of many words, as well as her intentional misspellings of words such as "goosez." Her use of z in place of s reflects the rule-breaking freedom and poetic license of her designs. Please see Jan's note on page 10.

The Five Angels, made by Jane Brinsden, Kaye Jacob, Deborah Claringbold, Jan Mullen, and Lee Mansbridge, 56" square, Perth, Western Australia, 1996.

Chapters 2 through 6 guide you through my wicked wayz. The techniques for making small units are presented first, followed by methods to transfer these ideas to blocks, and then you are shown how to easily resize these units and blocks. At the end of the technique chapters there are practice projects. The practice may be in the piecing—by making it just like mine, or you can choose to resize the blocks to create a bigger or smaller quilt.

In Chapter 7, Combining Techniques, I introduce you to the challenge of merging the techniques; that is, how to use two techniques or units in one block. It helps to read through these projects to understand how to change recipes to produce a different block focus.

You may also notice that there is some crooked logic in the content of some of the chapters. The chapter on Mainly Rectanglez has a triangle unit in it, and the chapter on Mainly Trianglez has a rectangle unit in it! These are placed according to technique and will help to extend the range of blocks you can make.

There are two other distinctive parts to my quilts that I share with you: my color and fabric choices, and the way I machine quilt most of my tops. Rather than go into color theory, I'll introduce you to my way of choosing and ordering fabrics by explaining my starting points and thoughts about color and fabric usage. I will also include some simple freehand machine quilting designs and mention why I chose them.

I hope you enjoy entering the new world of Stargazey Quilts in *Cut-Loose Quilts*...go forth, be colorful, cut crooked, and stitch happily!

CHAPTER 2

On the Crooked Path

Let's start the journey with some important definitions.

What does it mean to be "crooked" in Stargazey style? Stargazey quilts aren't crooked, the blocks we make aren't crooked, but the block divisions, or units, and sometimes the pieces we cut to make the units are usually crooked or skewed.

*"Pieces, units, blocks?" I hear you ask. A **piece** is a cut piece of fabric, not yet joined to another. A **unit** is a part of a block, usually pieced, which can also be used by itself as a block. A **block** is made up of units numbering between one and infinity! These blocks then join to make the **quilt body**. The **quilt top** is the body with borders attached and ready to sandwich and quilt. Phew!*

*In the technique chapters I use **unit** as the term for what we make, although often I could have called them blocks.*

TOOLS AND EQUIPMENT

The tools and equipment I use are not unusual, but I advise you to use good quality tools to make your patchwork and quilting more pleasurable. Make sure you have:

• A sewing machine to make these blocks. You need one that can produce a good straight stitch and, if possible, one with a 1/4" foot. If you want to quilt like I do, you will need a machine whose feed dogs can be dropped or covered, a walking foot, and a free-motion quilting foot, or an embroidery or darning foot.

• A rotary cutter, cutting mat, and at least one ruler are essential. I use a few different sized rulers in the course of making my quilt top. I cut large strips with a 6" x 24" ruler, smaller pieces with the 12" version, and would be lost without my 12 1/2" square for cutting background squares and squaring up the rough edges of crooked blocks.

• A heavy steam iron is great. Continuous ironing helps to keep the units and blocks flat and unstretched. When working in my crooked style, raw edges rarely have straight grain and these bias edges must be held well in check.

• My selection of pins suits the different processes I use them for. Generally I don't pin a lot during piecing, but if I do, I use long dressmakers' pins with a tiny head so the fabric sits as flat as possible at the machine. I use long yellow-headed quilters' pins around the edge of the quilt top when I sandwich, before I stabilize the edge with stitches sewn with the aid of a walking foot and before I begin the quilting process. Size 00 brass safety pins complete the tools for my machine quilting. I use these copiously for making channels for the walking foot to amble through, in the ditch, around the main divisions of blocks or units.

• Another tool that is very useful is a chalk wheel. I use mine when marking curved blocks and to mark out long freehand lines of quilting.

FABRICS

When I design patterns I list approximate fabric requirements, usually just a minimum yardage for focus fabrics and backgrounds. I don't want to limit you with the choices I made; I would rather you make the quilt **you** want, the size **you** want, the block size or sizes **you** want, the colors **you** want, the number of fabrics **you** want, the setting and the borders **you** want. Lots of decisions that will vary from person to person and quilt to quilt. I feel it best that I just give you guidelines.

You may also choose to change the fabric/color mix from my listed requirements. What is your block focus? What is your background? Does it have to look like my quilt? Choosing to concentrate on a different fabric mix you like makes for a quilt that reflects your style and personality. For example, the *Log Flowerz* quilt on page 65 has focus fabrics and background chosen to give the effect of flowers displayed in a garden. If I had chosen to use strips of the same focus fabrics and backgrounds, randomly placed, my quilt would be very different—same fabrics, alternate placement, unusual effect—a very unique quilt! Some of my quilts have one-color backgrounds, some have multicolored backgrounds, and others use the same fabrics alternating between the focus fabrics and backgrounds. Choose more, choose less, or just choose to do it your own way. An infinite variety can be created even within the same fabric palette.

A good starting point for your fabric choices is to begin with a color story and then gather fabric to build it. Sometimes one special fabric will be the initial inspiration, sometimes a photo in a magazine, or another quilt that you've seen and loved. I lay out the fabrics I am planning to use in runs of each color, to check that they all work together, continually adding and subtracting to add life and create the best mix. This simply involves neatly arranging fabrics from light to dark, showing equal amounts of a folded edge—an inch is usually enough. If a fabric

looks out of place at this stage it won't fit in later in the piecing process. If the mix is lacking brightness at this stage, now is the time to add those loud colors!

In the projects all yardage relates to 42" width. The amount specified is generous if you are using only one fabric, but if you are buying specifically for a project, and choosing many fabrics, you will need more (but you will have leftovers). I usually buy 1/2-yard cuts when I see something I like, so all my patterns work well with these cuts. Fat quarters or smaller cuts work with most patterns, too. It just depends on the block sizes you choose to work with. Remember all those choices?

I suggest building a healthy stash so you always have something on hand to add zing and variety when it is needed. If I run out of a certain fabric, it rarely worries me. It means that I must find a substitute, it stretches my abilities, and often makes for a more interesting quilt. Because I work with a maximum of 1/2-yard cuts and because I would rather use twenty reds than two reds, my fabric use has less preciousness, more interest, and surprisingly becomes much easier to work with.

I wash all my fabrics as soon as I get them home. I feel it is essential to wash fabrics before using them to get rid of excess dyes and chemicals, and, very importantly, to straighten the grain that may have been moved in the printing process. I also enjoy the time spent "cataloging" these new fabrics in my mind.

Because I want you to work freely I do not include requirements for binding or backing. I never decide on these until I am ready to use them and rarely buy anything special, choosing to use up the remaining fabrics from each quilt. The same goes for the border, too, although I do give you yardage requirements for these. Your quilt won't necessarily look good with the border I choose, so please don't cut borders until you need them.

My backings are usually made up with leftover pieces from the quilt top, perhaps combined with some bigger pieces bought especially for the quilt. I tend not to use math here—I merely lay the quilt top on the table or floor, then cover it with the pieces I have available. I then straighten their edges and sew them together until the back is at least three to four inches bigger around the edges than the top. This is a great way to use up leftover blocks, borders, sashings, or fabrics that you know you won't want to use again.

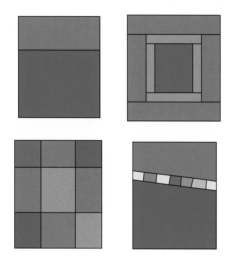

Some ideas for pieced backings

I often bind my quilts with leftover pieces from the quilt top, sometimes one fabric, sometimes three, sometimes small bits of many. If you are having trouble deciding on the perfect choice for your binding, go for more fabrics rather than less and let your eye do the blending. If the edge of the quilt needs a definite finish, choose a strong contrast in one fabric only. I use double-fold binding, and cut my binding strips 2" wide on the straight grain, to give a very tight fit. Bindings generally require a total of about $\frac{1}{2}$ yard of fabric.

I hope you are happy making these decisions. Taking your time at the start of a project is important; it is your fabric choices that will determine, above everything else, the successful eye appeal of your quilt!

CUTTING

I cut all fabrics with a rotary cutter and ruler. Accuracy is required in some cuts and with other cuts you have the freedom to cut roughly.

I CALL THIS ROUGH CUTTING THE "ISH" FACTOR. I WILL TELL YOU WHAT NEEDS TO BE EXACT, BUT WHEN YOU SEE AN "ISH" YOU KNOW IT DOESN'T HAVE TO BE PERFECT. IT MAY BE A BIT BIGGER OR A TINY BIT SMALLER OR CROOKED OR HAVE UNTRIMMED EDGES ON THE SIDES. DON'T VARY IT TOO MUCH, THOUGH, OR THE PATTERN MAY NEED ADJUSTING.

SOME TECHNIQUES REQUIRE STACKING AT LEAST TWO FABRICS AND SUBSEQUENT FABRIC SWAPPING. ONCE AGAIN, YOU WILL BE TOLD WHEN TO DO THIS. OTHERWISE, YOU MAY STACK AND CUT PURELY TO SAVE TIME. STACKED FABRICS ARE ILLUSTRATED SLIGHTLY OFFSET, BUT SHOULD BE STACKED EXACTLY ON TOP OF EACH OTHER WHEN CUTTING.

When you need to square up a finished block I suggest you use a square ruler the size you need, or use a 12$\frac{1}{2}$" square ruler with masking tape placed on the edge of the correct measurements as a guideline. If you haven't yet invested in a large square ruler, use the markings on your cutting mat. Trimming at the end leads to accurate block sizes which, when joined together, make a more perfect quilt top. Easy!

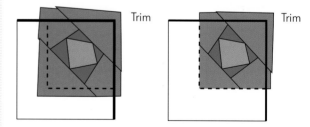

Trimming a square using a square ruler

PIECING

In most cases I suggest using an accurate ¼" seam, but sometimes I let you get away with just a straight seam using the "ish" factor again. If you see the "ish" you have permission to relax and slap on these pieces!

I always chain piece to save time and keep order throughout both unit and block making, as well as the piecing of the quilt body. Laying and/or stacking block pieces in order next to your sewing machine and then replacing them in their correct position after pressing will help you keep that order.

Working with pieces or units that are angular or irregular causes potential problems, just as it does in traditional patchwork. To join pieces like these so the edges run in a straight—not stepped—line, the outer edges need to cross exactly on the seam lines. I call this the crossover point. I give you a couple of ways to easily obtain this straight edge depending on the block you are making.

Option 1. If the pieces are equal in length, crooked, and sliced in only one direction (for example, the Three-Patchez unit on page 16), align the edges, then move the pieces until the two top and the two bottom edges intersect exactly ¼" in from the seam edges.

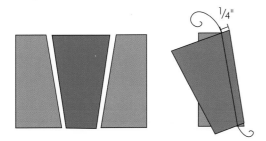

Stitching crooked pieces with a crossover point in detail

With units that are sliced in both directions, such as Four-Patchez and Nine-Patchez, the inner points often do not meet perfectly because of the angular nature of the pieces, which would traditionally require extra in the seam allowance.

Option 2. For Four-Patchez, I usually make sure that the outer edges of the blocks cross over perfectly and let what will be the inner seam edges of the block cross where they will.

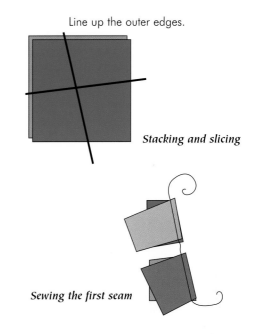

Line up the outer edges.

Stacking and slicing

Sewing the first seam

The second seam will be lined up to get the outer edges sitting perfectly, but that means that the points may not meet perfectly in the center. The seam edges may be uneven, and you must use the "average" of the seam as the stitching line. These edges will probably be stepped, and the seam allowance may vary from ⅛"- to ¼"-ish in places.

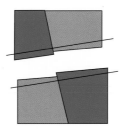

Stitching line for Four-Patchez second seam

Option 3. For Nine-Patchez, I line up the center row pieces so the crossover points are averaged out and the top and bottom row pieces are treated the same way as the Four-Patchez in Option 2.

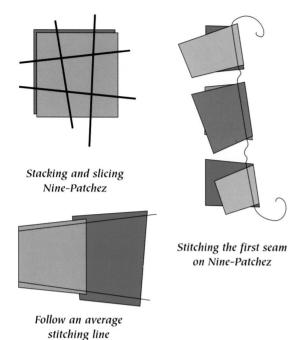

Stacking and slicing Nine-Patchez

Stitching the first seam on Nine-Patchez

Follow an average stitching line

Option 4. Another way to approach these awkward pieces, especially if they are very crooked, is to choose to add an extra inch to two sides before cutting out, and then squaring up the block later. If you choose this method, the crossover points that you want to match well are the inner ones, not the outer edges, as in the previous options. The outer edges are trimmed off anyway.

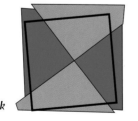

Squaring up a Cross-Patchez block

PRESSING

I press after stitching every seam and do it gently, yet firmly, from the front to make sure the fabric stays true to size and shape. In these crooked blocks, the straight grain is in funny places, trying not to do funny things, so it is very important that you don't stretch the fabric.

I generally press the seams under the focus fabrics or the main focus of the block to suit the way I machine quilt. By doing this, I am trying to accentuate the main focus of the block. The slight bulk of the seams, combined with stitching around the main focus in the ditch, and heavily free-motion quilting the background, does push out the unquilted main focus fabrics.

In blocks where seams cross, such as Nine-Patchez, it is best to press one seam right and one seam left, usually toward the darker fabric, to help them nest sweetly together later.

I usually press fabric toward the inner borders to give them a strong line.

MACHINE QUILTING

My quilting style has developed from the desire to be able to "draw" individual details rather than always working in a continuous line with the design limitations that this imposes. As long as the ends of each motif are well secured, there are no problems about "drawing" anything you like. To be able to achieve the results I wanted, I have devised ways of working to help me create work that is flat, interesting in detail, and fun to do.

I use small safety pins when sandwiching my quilts—lots of them—placed in a way that creates a channel on either side of my chosen ditch quilting track. These pins are placed about 1" apart. I very rarely mark the quilt top, preferring to sketch designs to scale on paper. "If you can draw it, you can—with practice—quilt it freehand" is my quilting battle-cry!

I stabilize the edges of the quilt using the walking foot and a large stitch approximately $1/8$" in from the outer edge to eliminate edge/border wonkiness. I quilt in-the-ditch around the blocks, units, and pieces that I want to stand out. Usually this is the main design of a block, the borders, and the sashings. Out come all the pins, then I heavily free-motion machine-quilt the backgrounds to focus attention on the main designs even more.

I start and stop the quilting with either very, very tiny stitches or minute backstitches, and usually jump between motifs, always ending off and starting again, rather than stitching to the next motif in continuous lines. At regular intervals I take the quilt sandwich off the machine and trim the top jumping threads back to the start and end of each motif with thread clippers. The quilt gets flipped over, and I then clip the lower jumping threads off, giving a small tug on each thread to pull the cut ends to the back.

Trim threads between motifs.

Jumping between motifs

I prefer to use cotton thread for piecing, but for free-motion quilting I choose polyester, for both its strength and for the color choices. I try to hide the thread on the fabric and give the impression of textures and shadows with my stitching. Choose a color as close as possible to the fabric or darker than it. I will show you what simple motifs I have used with these quilts, but I encourage you to turn your own doodles into simple quilting patterns.

Now you are ready to take the leap toward cutting into some fabric and perhaps resizing some blocks. Please remember that **it is very important that you make up a sample block in each size unit or block that you plan to use before you jump into making a whole quilt.** I use unusual methods that may require some personal adaptation, be it in the sizing, the cutting, or the piecing. I offer you freedom, but I urge you to take your time. Take a deep breath...and have FUN!

 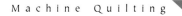

CHAPTER 3

Mainly Rectanglez

It's almost mandatory for people to begin their quiltmaking life by making a quilt based on the simple and logical geometric forms of squares and rectangles. We like the look of those simple quilts and we enjoy the straightforward play of color and print. We think—I could do that! It is precisely there that I start guiding you along my crooked path. Squares and rectangles that are broken by skewed or crooked lines can have that same simple appeal and are no harder to make than traditional ones. All the units in this chapter rely on a stack of **at least** two fabrics. These are sliced through at an angle you choose, and the pieces are switched and then resewn along the cut. **Stack, slice, switch,** and **sew—simple!**

I show you how to make Two-Patchez, Three-Patchez, Four-Patchez, Six-Patchez, Nine-Patchez, and Cross-Patchez units and indicate how you can modify or extend the ideas behind all these. You can then make up one of the quilts at the end of the chapter, or if you are feeling inspired, confident, and creative, you may modify a traditional pattern that incorporates one or more of these units.

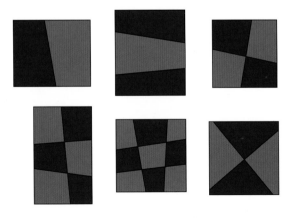

In this chapter please remember:

- All slices are cut in straight lines with a rotary cutter and ruler.

- All sewing must be done with an accurate $1/4"$ seam to bring the blocks back to the correct size.

- All the blocks in this chapter rely on a stack of two fabrics to work, but you end up with two blocks as a bonus!

- All the blocks can have their inner or outer proportions changed; they can be squished or elongated in various directions without the math of the blocks changing.

- Each of these blocks can be made as a square or a rectangle.

- With units that are sliced in both directions, such as Four-Patchez, Six-Patchez, and Nine-Patchez, sometimes the points do not meet perfectly because of the triangular nature of the pieces, which would traditionally require extra in the seam allowance. See page 11 for the appropriate piecing guidelines.

Are you ready? Let's get started. I encourage you to take out some scraps and make a sample block of each with me to turn theory into practice...

TWO-PATCHEZ UNIT

This is the easiest of units to do, a great place to begin, not fancy, but very useful as a filler or border unit.

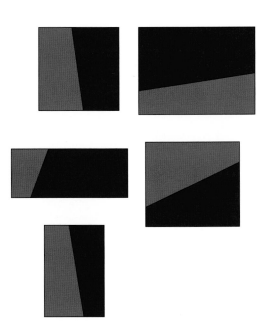

Cutting Recipe for a Pair of Two-Patchez Units

1. Decide on the finished size of the units.

2. Add $1/4$" all around.

3. Add another $1/2$" along the side that will be sliced.

An Example

1. I need a 3" x 6" finished rectangle.

2. I add $1/4$" all around, which brings the rectangle to $3^1/2$" x $6^1/2$".

Adding the seam allowance

3. I add $1/2$" as shown. I cut two rectangles 4" x $6^1/2$", which will be sliced through once.

Adding $1/2$" per slice

Piecing a Pair of Two-Patchez Units

1. Stack two squares/rectangles exactly on top of each other, right sides up.

2. Slice through these squares/rectangles at an angle.

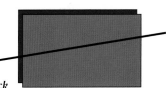

Slicing the stack

3. Switch the two right-hand pieces as you place both blocks on the table.

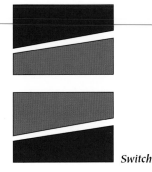

Switching the pieces

4. Sew both units back together along the slice.

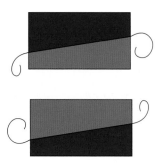

Sewing the pieces together

Easy, wasn't it? Now let's step slowly forward with the...

THREE-PATCHEZ UNIT

Once again, not a spectacular block in itself, but very useful as a component of others.

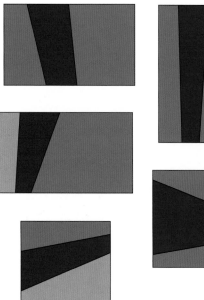

Cutting Recipe for a Pair of Three-Patchez Units

1. Decide on the finished size of the units.

2. Add $1/4$" all around.

3. Add another 1" to the side that will be sliced ($1/2$" per slice).

An Example

1. I need a 6" finished square.

2. I add $1/4$" all around, which brings the square to $6\frac{1}{2}$" x $6\frac{1}{2}$".

Adding the seam allowance

3. I add 1" as shown, which means that I cut two rectangles $6\frac{1}{2}$" x $7\frac{1}{2}$", which will be sliced through twice.

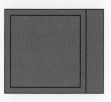

Adding $1/2$" per slice for a total of 1" extra

Piecing a Pair of Three-Patchez Units

1. Stack the two squares/rectangles exactly on top of each other, right sides up.

2. Slice twice down the length/width so the divisions are roughly in thirds but are skewed.

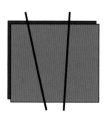

Slicing the stack

3. Switch the two middle pieces as you place both units on the table.

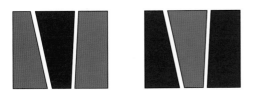

Switching the pieces

4. Working on both units, sew the left and middle pieces together on both units.

Sewing the pieces together

5. Sew the left sections and the right piece together.

A complete unit

The next step is to learn to slice and restitch in both directions. Doing this requires that you make some decisions according to the severity of the angles you cut. If your slices aren't very crooked you need to follow the piecing Options 2 or 3 on pages 11 and 12. If you do want severe angles you may choose to add the "extra crooked allowance" of Option 4 on page 12, and trim the block down to the correct unfinished size at the end, as I always do to make the Cross-Patchez units.

Remember, though, above all else, we are more interested in quirky than perfect!

FOUR-PATCHEZ UNIT

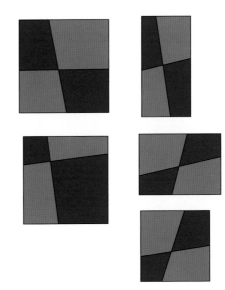

Cutting Recipe for a Pair of Four-Patchez Units

1. Decide on the finished size of the units.

2. Add ¼" all around.

3. Add another ½" for each slice. (If you need to, add the "extra crooked allowance" of 1"-ish all around.)

An Example

1. I need a 4" finished square.

2. I add ¼" all around, which brings the square to 4½" square.

Adding the seam allowance

3. I add ½" in each direction as shown, which means that I cut two 5" squares.

Adding ½" per slice in two directions

Piecing a Pair of Four-Patchez Units

1. Stack the two squares/rectangles exactly on top of each other, right sides up.

2. Slice down the length and then again carefully across the width without disturbing the pieces.

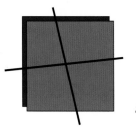

Slicing the stack

3. Switch two opposing pieces as you place both units on the table.

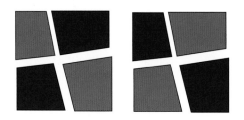

Switching the pieces

4. Working on both units, sew the two top pieces together, then sew the two bottom pieces together, preferably in a chain.

Sewing the pieces together

5. Stitch these two sections together.

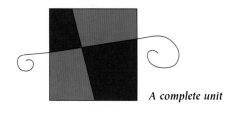

A complete unit

6. If you have added the "extra crooked cutting allowance," trim the units to the correct unfinished size.

The Six-Patchez unit goes just one slice further, but it is a unit I often use in borders.

SIX-PATCHEZ UNIT

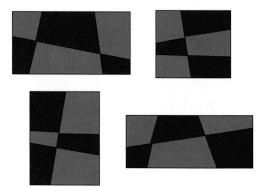

Cutting Recipe for a Pair of Six-Patchez Units

1. Decide on the finished size of the units.

2. Add ¹/₄" all around.

3. Add another ¹/₂" along the side to be sliced once, add 1" along the side to be sliced twice. (If you need to, add the "extra crooked allowance" of 1"-ish all around.) The example that follows shows you where to add the "extras."

An Example

1. I need a 4" x 6" finished rectangle.

2. I add ¼" all around, which brings the rectangle to 4½" x 6½".

3. I add ½" to the side to be sliced once, and add 1" to the side to be sliced twice. I cut two rectangles 5" x 7½".

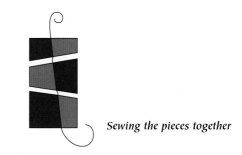

Adding the seam allowance

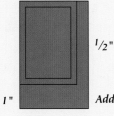

½"

1"   *Adding ½" per slice*

Piecing a Pair of Six-Patchez Units

1. Stack the two squares/rectangles exactly on top of each other, right sides up.

2. Slice down the length and then again carefully across the width, in two places, without disturbing the pieces.

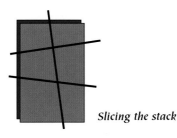

Slicing the stack

3. Switch three opposing pieces as you place both units on the table.

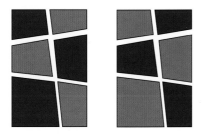

Switching the pieces

4. Working with both units, sew the two top pieces together. Feed and sew the two middle pieces together. Feed and sew the two bottom pieces together.

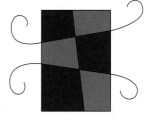

Sewing the pieces together

5. Sew two sections together. Repeat for the last seam.

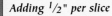

A complete unit

6. If you have added the "extra crooked cutting allowance," trim the units to the correct unfinished size.

And then it becomes a bit trickier...

NINE-PATCHEZ UNIT

The difficulty here is not the cutting or the piecing, necessarily, it is the traditional desire to get those points to meet PERFECTLY. Learn to relax a little.

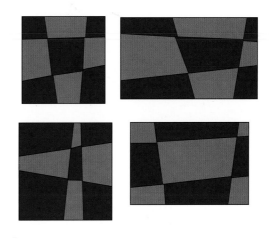

Cutting Recipe for a Pair of Nine-Patchez Units

1. Decide on the finished size of the units.

2. Add ¼" all around.

3. Add another 1" in two directions as shown below. (If you need to, add the "extra crooked allowance" of 1"-ish all around.)

An Example

1. I need a 6" finished square.

2. I add ¼" all around, which brings the square to 6½".

3. I add 1" in two directions, which means that I cut two 7½" squares.

Adding the seam allowance

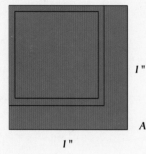

Adding 1" total on two sides

Piecing a Pair of Nine-Patchez Units

1. Stack the two squares/rectangles exactly on top of each other, right sides up.

2. Slice twice in both directions without disturbing the pieces.

Slicing the stack

3. Switch four opposing pieces as you place both units on the table.

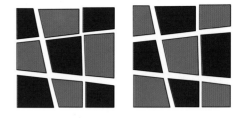

Switching the pieces

4. Working on both units, sew the top left and top center pieces. Feed and sew the middle left and middle center pieces. Feed and sew the bottom left and bottom center pieces. Repeat this process sewing the right pieces onto the left center sections.

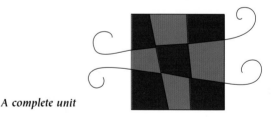

Sewing the pieces together

5. Sew two of the sections together, nesting the seams, if possible. Repeat for the last seam.

A complete unit

6. If you have added the "extra crooked cutting allowance," trim the blocks to the correct unfinished size.

Now the last of the rectangles units, the Cross-Patchez unit, looks like it belongs in the triangles chapter. This unit illustrates the use of the "extra crooked cutting allowance" and is especially useful if you would like to make an Ohio Starz block.

CROSS-PATCHEZ UNIT

This is just a very crooked Four-Patchez unit. Different techniques are needed, though, to account for the extra take-up of the severe angles.

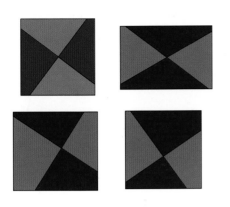

Cutting Recipe for a Pair of Cross-Patchez Units

1. Decide on the finished size of the units.

2. Add $1/4$" all around.

3. Add another $1/2$" in two directions.

4. Add the "extra crooked allowance" of 1"-ish on two sides.

An Example

1. I need a 5" finished square.

2. I add $1/4$" all around, which brings the square to $5^1/2$".

3. I add $1/2$" in on two sides, which brings the square to 6".

Adding the seam allowance

4. I add the "extra crooked allowance" of 1"-ish as shown below, which means that I cut two 7"-ish squares.

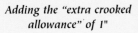
Adding $1/2$" per slice

Adding the "extra crooked allowance" of 1"

Piecing a Pair of Cross-Patchez Units

1. Stack the two squares/rectangles exactly on top of each other, right sides up.

2. Slice from corner-ish to corner-ish in both directions without disturbing the pieces.

Slicing the stack

3. Switch two opposing pieces as you place both units on the table.

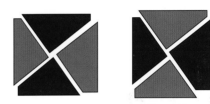
Switching the pieces

4. Working on both units, sew two adjacent pieces together, making sure the seam lines cross over at the center. Ignore the uneven outer edges. Feed and sew the other two adjacent pieces together, crossing at the center as before.

Sewing the pieces

5. Sew both sections together, nesting the seams, and matching the centers.

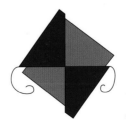
Sewing the sections together

6. Trim the units to the unfinished size.

Squaring up the unit

EXTENDING THE RECTANGLEZ OPTIONS

Fabric Choices

All the blocks in this chapter must be stack-cut from at least two fabrics, but if you cut from more fabrics you will increase your design and color options, and end up with more blocks as a result. For example, a set of Three-Patchez units cut from three fabrics gives you three blocks.

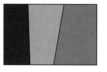

Three-Patchez in three fabrics

A set of Three-Patchez units cut from four fabrics gives you four blocks.

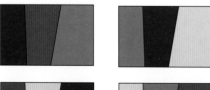

Three-Patchez in four fabrics

I usually cut from a maximum stack of six fabrics as the accuracy of the cuts diminishes as the stack gets higher.

Extra Patchez

I've shown you how to cut Four-Patchez, Six-Patchez, and Nine-Patchez units. Why stop there? What about Sixteen-Patchez and Twenty-Five-Patchez made by working in the same vein and adding an extra ¹/₂" per slice?

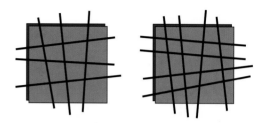

Stacking and slicing Sixteen-Patchez and Twenty-Five-Patchez

Changing the Style of an Inner Unit

We can change the insides of the unit by

squishing

stretching

and poking into corners

all without changing the recipe!

Changing the Shape of the Outer Edge

Of course the shape of the outer edge can be changed, too. You wouldn't want to work out the math, though. I suggest just cutting a stack of the same shape, slicing, restitching, and then trimming the outer edge. It's a challenge to piece these in a quilt top, but they could be squared up by adding sashing strips and then trimming to size.

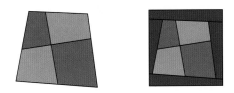

Odd-shaped Four-Patchez — naked and bordered

Using a Cut Piece as a Template

If you would like to replace one piece with another, you may use your initial sliced piece as a template. This means that you can use up that special tiny bit of fabric, or if you make a mistake you can replace the "bad" piece or pieces.

Let's try it with Four-Patchez; perhaps you would like one of the striped pieces to face the other direction? Simply lay your new striped fabric on the cutting mat right side up and in the correct direction. Place the "wrong" piece on top right side up and cut a duplicate piece using a rotary cutter and ruler. This opens up great possibilities for adding in scraps and zapping up blocks that are looking a bit plain.

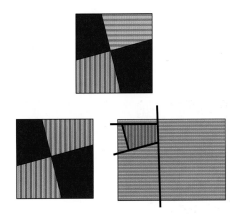

Using a sliced piece as a template

Making Roman Stripez Like Mine

Roman Stripez by Jan Mullen, 43$^1/2$" x 53$^1/2$", 1999.

UNITS/TECHNIQUES USED

Three-Patchez units for the quilt body are combined

with Three-Patchez units and Vertical Four-Patchez units in the border.

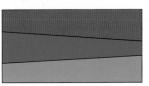

Refer to the cutting and piecing instructions for Three-Patchez units on page 16. For the Vertical Four-Patchez in the border an extra 1¹/₂" was added, since you make three slices.

COLOR STORY

This gentle quilt reminds me of the sea. It started with a few aquas and blues, and I built up eye appeal when I was playing with the fabrics by adding the purples, greens, and hints of buttery yellows. A few strong prints helped blend the colors. Usually a Roman Stripe block has a light center and two dark sides, but I chose to keep colors well mixed by working with sets of three different fabrics per block.

Quilt Size: 43¹/₂" x 53¹/₂"

Block Size and Set: Blocks are 5" square, set seven by nine for a total of sixty-three blocks.

FABRIC REQUIREMENTS

Blocks/Outer Border Blocks = 3¹/₂ yards of assorted greens, blues, aquas, purples, and yellows

Inner Border = ¹/₄ yard of assorted blues

CUTTING & PIECING THE QUILT BODY

Cut sixty-three 5¹/₂" x 6¹/₂" rectangles. Stack in sets of three coordinating colors.

Slicing the stack

Follow the piecing instructions for Three-Patchez units on page 16. Arrange, alternating their direction. Sew together to form the quilt body.

INNER BORDERS

Sides: Piece and cut two strips 1¹/₂" x 45¹/₂". Sew to the quilt body.

Top and bottom: Piece and cut two strips 1¹/₂" x 37¹/₂". Sew to the quilt body.

OUTER BORDERS

This border is made of five different sized/directioned Three-Patchez and Vertical Four-Patchez units that continue the alternating effect we started in the quilt body. Follow the piecing instructions for Three-Patchez. Slice as shown.

Unit 1 Three-Patchez

Cut twelve 4¹/₂" x 5¹/₂" rectangles. Work with four sets of three fabrics. When finished these units measure 3" x 5".

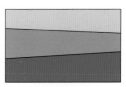

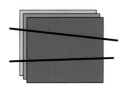

Stacking and slicing Unit 1

Unit 2 Three-Patchez

Cut twelve 3½" x 6½" rectangles. Work with four sets of three fabrics. When finished these units measure 3" x 5".

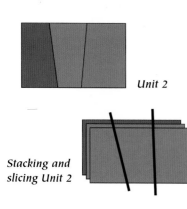

Unit 2

Stacking and slicing Unit 2

Unit 3 Three-Patchez

Cut four 4½" x 6½" rectangles. Work with one set of four fabrics. When finished these units measure 3" x 6".

Unit 3

Stacking and slicing Unit 3

Unit 4 Vertical Four-Patchez

Cut four 3½" x 8" rectangles. Work with one set of four fabrics. When finished these units measure 3" x 6".

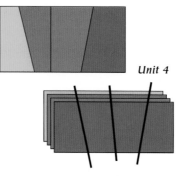

Unit 4

Stacking and slicing Unit 4

Unit 5 Three-Patchez

Cut four 3½" x 4½" rectangles. Work with one set of four fabrics. When finished these units measure 3" square.

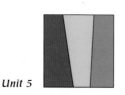

Unit 5

Stacking and slicing Unit 5

Sew together side sections as shown. Sew to the quilt body.

| 3 | 2 | 1 | 2 | 1 | 2 | 1 | 2 | 3 |

Layout for side borders

Sew together the top and bottom sections as shown. Sew to the quilt body.

| 5 | 4 | 1 | 2 | 1 | 2 | 1 | 4 | 5 |

Layout for top and bottom borders

MACHINE QUILTING

Detail of Roman Stripez

Continuing with the sea theme, I felt this top needed lots of curly seaweed, starfish, and assorted undersea shapes to counteract the strong linear effect of these repeat blocks. I left the center piece unquilted in every block to keep it feeling cuddly.

Undersea quilting themes

Current Check-Outs summary for Schuster,
Mon Oct 18 16:34:25 EDT 2010

BARCODE: 35099002933951
TITLE: Sisterhood [videorecording DVD] /
DUE DATE: Oct 25 2010

BARCODE: 35099000050873
TITLE: A cure for dreams : a novel / Kay
DUE DATE: Nov 15 2010

BARCODE: 35099001599100
TITLE: The twisted root / Anne Perry
DUE DATE: Nov 15 2010

BARCODE: 35099002579952
TITLE: Olive kitteridge / Elizabeth Stro
DUE DATE: Nov 15 2010

Making Nine-Patchez Like Mine

Nine-Patchez on Point by Jan Mullen, 53" x 70", 1999.

UNITS/TECHNIQUES USED

Nine-Patchez units

For the border, Four-Patchez units, Six-Patchez units, and Eight-Patchez units are used.

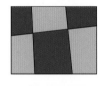

Refer to the cutting and piecing instructions for Four-Patchez units, Six-Patchez units, and Nine-Patchez units on pages 17-19. For the Eight-Patchez unit in the border you will need to follow the Six-Patchez unit cutting and piecing instructions, but add an extra 1/2" and make an extra slice.

COLOR STORY

I wanted this quilt to fit well on a bed and be quiet enough to not dominate a room—not my usual way of working! Lots of yellows as backgrounds, and oranges, pinks, and reds as the main focus were plucked from the shelves with the idea of using both dull and bright pieces of each color as another way to tone down my usual upbeat inclinations.

Quilt Size: 53" x 70"

Block Size and Set: Blocks are 6" square, set five by seven for a total of thirty-five blocks.

FABRIC REQUIREMENTS

Backgrounds = 3 1/2 yards of assorted yellows for the quilt body and border

Focus Fabrics = 2 1/2 yards of assorted oranges, pinks, and reds for the quilt body and border

Inner Border = 1/3 yard of assorted reds

CUTTING & PIECING THE QUILT BODY

Nine-Patchez Blocks

Cut thirty-six 7 1/2" squares — eighteen backgrounds and eighteen focus fabrics. Stack, slice, switch, and sew them in nine sets each containing two backgrounds and two focus fabrics. This will make thirty-six blocks; discard the one you like least to bring the number back to the required thirty-five.

Background Squarez

Cut twenty-four 6 1/2" squares from background fabrics.

Background Side Trianglez

Cut five 9 3/4" squares from background fabrics. Slice them in quarters from corner to corner.

Corner Trianglez

Cut two 5 1/8" squares from background fabric. Slice them in half from corner to corner.

Arrange the blocks, background squares, and triangles on point as shown in the photo. Piece in diagonal rows, then piece the rows together.

INNER BORDERS

Sides: Piece and cut two strips 1 1/2" x 60". Sew to the quilt body.

Top and bottom: Piece and cut two 1 1/2" x 45" strips. Sew to the quilt body.

OUTER BORDERS

The outer borders follow the basic Four-Patchez and Six-Patchez recipes, but as I set the Nine-Patchez on point, I also added Eight-Patchez units for a more continuous flow around the quilt body.

Unit 1 Four-Patchez

Cut four 5" squares—two from backgrounds and two from focus fabrics. Stack, slice, switch, and sew them all in one set. You will use these four 4" square units for the corners.

Unit 2 Eight-Patchez

Cut twenty-four 5" x 10½" rectangles—twelve from backgrounds and twelve from focus fabrics. Stack, slice, switch, and sew them as Eight-Patchez units in six sets each containing two backgrounds and two focus fabrics. You will make twenty-four 4" x 8½" units, but only use twenty of them for the sides. The extras are necessary to make a continuous checkerboard pattern, and can be used in the backing.

Unit 3 Six-Patchez

Cut eight 5" x 6¾" rectangles— four from backgrounds and four from focus fabrics. Stack, slice, switch, and sew them in two sets each containing two backgrounds and two focus fabrics.

You will make eight 4" x 5¼" units for the inner corners. Sew the side units together as shown. Sew to the quilt body.

3	2	2	2	2	2	2	3

Layout for side borders

Sew the top/bottom units together as shown. Sew to the quilt body.

1	3	2	2	2	2	3	1

Layout for top and bottom borders

MACHINE QUILTING

Detail of Nine-Patchez on Point

In an effort to keep it simple for a "quiet" bed quilt, I decided to quilt over all of the vacant blocks with daisies. I love the freehand "drawn" petals multiplied to form a delicate pattern.

4 blue
4 colored
4 green
2 purple

Ohio Starz by Jan Mullen, 42¹/₂" x 60¹/₂", 1999.

UNITS/TECHNIQUES USED

Cross-Patchez units that

make up the Ohio Starz block are also used as borders.

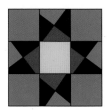

Refer to the cutting and piecing instructions for Cross-Patchez on page 21.

COLOR STORY

I wanted to use jewel colors here to contrast with black star points. Another goal was to get different mixes of these colors so I used three within each block. To make the block look more crooked than mine, the centers and inner triangles of the Cross-Patchez could be of the same color or fabric.

Quilt Size: 42½" x 60½"

Block Size and Set: Blocks are 9" square, set four by six for a total of twenty-four blocks.

The Cross-Patchez units in the blocks are 3"; ninety-six units needed.

FABRIC REQUIRE-MENTS

Star Points/Border Units = 1¾ yards of assorted blacks

Backgrounds/Inner Points/Star Centers/Border Units = 3½ yards of assorted colors

CUTTING & PIECING THE QUILT BODY

Cross-Patchez Units

Cut ninety-six 5"-ish squares— forty-eight blacks and forty-eight from assorted colors. Stack, slice, switch, and sew them into twenty-four sets, each containing two blacks for the star point, one background and one inner point. Each block will use a set of four Cross-Patchez units.

Ohio Starz Blocks

Cut twenty-four 3½" squares for the center of each block.

Cut ninety-six 3½" squares. Sets of four are needed as corners to match the backgrounds of the Cross-Patchez in each block.

Arrange the Cross-Patchez sets with a center and a background block set.

Stitch together the twenty-four blocks.

Arrange the completed blocks together. Sew together to form the quilt body.

BORDERS

You will need sixty-four Cross-Patchez units.

Cut sixty-four 5"-ish squares— thirty-two black and thirty-two colored.

Group into sixteen sets of four, each containing two blacks and two assorted colors.

Set aside one group to make the corner units. Stack, slice, switch, and sew these with the two blacks and the two colors adjacent to help the border flow around the corners.

Corner units

Stack, slice, switch, and sew the other fifteen sets with blacks and colors opposite as for the blocks.

Sew eighteen units together for the two sides. Sew to the quilt body.

Sew twelve units together for the top and bottom. Sew on a corner unit to each end. Sew to the quilt body.

MACHINE QUILTING

Detail of Ohio Starz

I also kept the quilting very simple here. Curls, one of my favorite fillers, speedily covered the background fabrics and the colored areas of the border. Everything else is stitched in-the-ditch to keep the layers together.

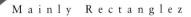

CHAPTER 4

Mainly Trianglez

Working with squares and rectangles is normally the first step in traditional patchwork, but most quilters want to quickly move on to more intricate shapes and patterns. Then you turn to triangles, each type differentiated by their different cut, angle, or function. These are generally acknowledged as a bit tricky or "fiddly;" some people even go out of their way to avoid them. In the liberated Stargazey style we must have triangles; too small, too large, floating, no points, and definitely crooked. There is no reason to run and hide!

In this chapter we have triangles in one corner, triangles in two corners, triangles in four corners, or triangles making a run of it up the middle of a rectangle. This "covering corners" technique can also be useful when dealing with rectangles too.

Let me sum up this chapter and get you sewing triangles in my relaxed style by saying "the point here is **not** the point!"

In this chapter please remember:

- All slices are cut in straight lines with a rotary cutter and ruler. Not all the pieces have to be cut perfectly—the measurements followed by an "-ish" can be approximate.

- Sewing the cut slices together must be done with an accurate $1/4$" seam (see Option 1, page 11, for how to do this).

- Sewing on the triangle pieces doesn't have to be so fussy. Like the squares they are cut from, an "-ish" measurement can be used.

- Each time you cover a corner, gently fold it back before stitching to make sure that the corner underneath will be properly covered.

- Always press the covered corners open before trimming the excess triangle fabric.

- All the blocks can have their inner or outer proportions changed.

- All the blocks can be made as a square or a rectangle.

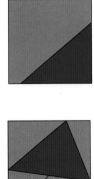

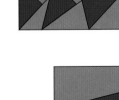

Here we go...

COVER CORNER TRIANGLEZ UNIT

Use these units instead of half-square triangles in traditional blocks. You can make a whole quilt with this unit alone, but it's most useful as a part of a block.

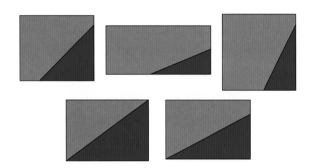

Cutting Recipe for a Cover Corner Trianglez Unit

1. Decide on the finished size of the unit.

2. Add ¼" all around and cut a background piece this size.

3. Cut a square of triangle fabric 1"-ish bigger than the cut background square, and slice this in half-ish from corner to corner. Use only one triangle.

An Example

1. I need a 3" square finished unit.

2. I add ¼" all around, which means I cut the background 3½" square.

Adding the seam allowance

3. I cut a 4½"-ish square of triangle fabric and slice this in half-ish from corner to corner. I use only one of these cut triangles.

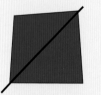

Slicing into triangles

Piecing a Cover Corner Trianglez Unit

1. Place the background square right side up and place the triangle in the position you desire, also right side up. I generally place the triangle below the center diagonal of the background square and vary its position from unit to unit. You can also go above the center diagonal if you like, but the triangle must, when stitched and pressed, cover the edges of the background piece.

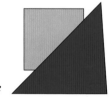

Auditioning the triangle

2. Flip the triangle over so the pieces are right sides together, at the same time pulling it toward the corner a little to allow for the seam allowance. Stitch and press.

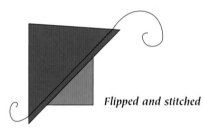

Flipped and stitched

3. With right sides down, trim the triangle edges even with the background piece.

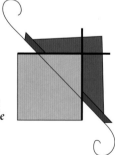

Trimming the added triangle

4. Flip the unit over, pull back the triangle, and trim the excess background fabric even with the seam allowance.

Trim line

Trimming the excess

A complete unit!

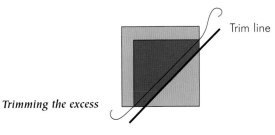

With an understanding of covering corners we can move on and make more involved units. Let's march toward our...

MELON PATCHEZ UNIT

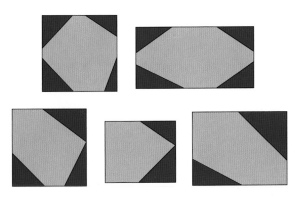

The Melon Patchez unit extends the method of covered corner triangles. Here the background square is usually a lot larger and has all the corners covered, generally without overlap. We don't have to follow tradition; we may decide not to cover all the corners of the background square, choose to have the triangles/corners overlapping, or make them more severe. However, be prepared to cut the squares larger when cutting the triangles fabric to allow for more coverage.

Cutting Recipe for a Melon Patchez Unit

1. Decide on the finished size of the block.

2. Add ¼" all around and cut the background to this size.

3. Cut two squares from triangle fabric approximately half the finished length of the background piece plus a 1"-ish cutting allowance. Slice these squares in half-ish from corner to corner.

An Example

1. I need a 6" finished square.

2. I add ¼" all around, which means I cut my background 6½" square.

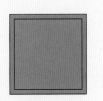

Adding the seam allowance

3. I cut two 4"-ish squares from triangle fabric. I slice them in half-ish from corner to corner.

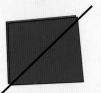

Slicing the 4"-ish squares into triangles

Piecing a Melon Patchez Unit

1. Place the background square right side up, place the first triangle in the position you desire, also right side up. Try to vary its position in subsequent corners.

Trying out the triangle placement

2. Flip the triangle over so the pieces are right sides together, at the same time pulling it toward the corner a little to allow for the seam allowance. Stitch and press.

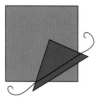

Flipped and stitched

3. With right sides down, trim the triangle edges even with the background square.

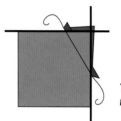

Trimming even with the background

4. Flip the unit over, pull back the triangle, and trim the excess background fabric even with the seam allowance.

Trimming the excess

A complete corner!

5. Repeat for the other three corners to finish the unit.

Melon Patchez with all corners covered

Now we'll cover the corners more completely with a . . .

SINGLE FLYING GOOSEZ UNIT

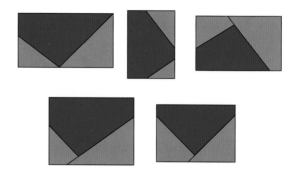

This unit makes a great quilt on its own, but is also wonderful combined with other units to make blocks like Sawtooth Starz. Made with cover corner techniques, these Flying Goosez—single, double, and multiple—are deliciously quirky and easy as pie.

In the traditional unit, the length is equal to twice the width. My recipes are devised with this proportion in mind. The cutting for the goosez must be accurate but the backgrounds can be rough. **Using my techniques you actually add the background triangles to the goosez fabric.**

Cutting Recipe for a Single Flying Goosez Unit

1. Decide on the finished size of the unit.

2. Add 1/4" all around and cut a goosez piece to this measurement.

3. Cut a square the finished length of the goosez piece from background fabric, and slice it in half-ish from corner to corner.

An Example

1. I want a finished unit 3" x 6".

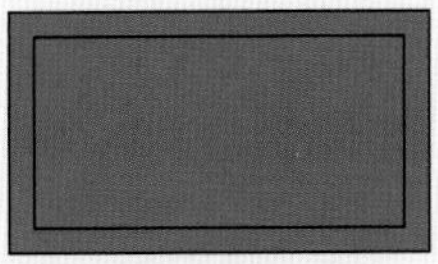

Adding the seam allowance

2. I add 1/4" all around and cut a goosez piece 3 1/2" x 6 1/2".

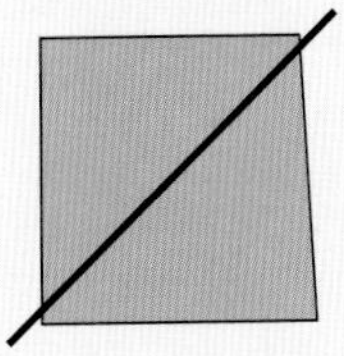

3. I cut a 6"-ish square of background fabric and slice it in half-ish from corner to corner.

Slicing into triangles

Piecing a Single Flying Goosez Unit

1. With the goosez piece right side up, place the first background triangle in the position you desire, also right side up. I generally vary its position from unit to unit: some starting left, on, or right of center, some over, some on, and some under the corner.

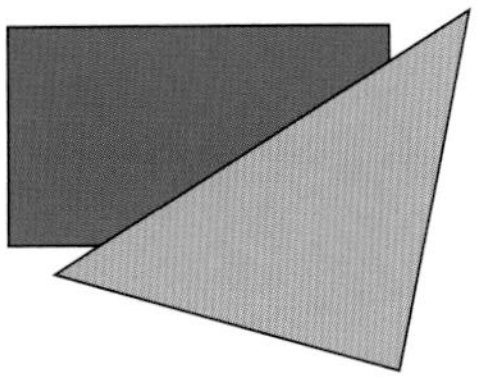

Testing the triangle

2. Flip the triangle over so the pieces are right sides together, at the same time pulling it toward the corner to allow for the seam allowance. Stitch.

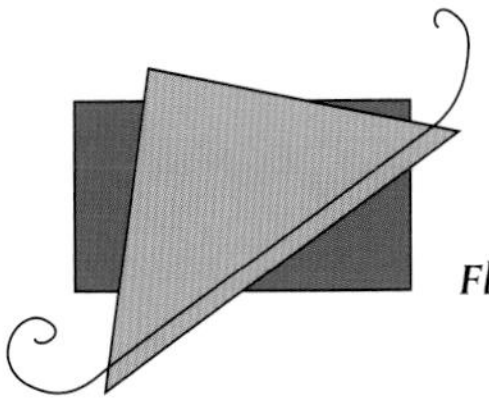

Flipping and stitching

3. With right sides down, trim the triangle edges even with the goosez piece.

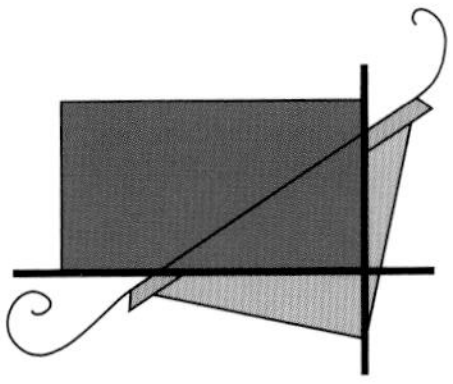

Trimming even with the goosez piece

4. Flip the unit over, pull back the triangle, and trim the excess background fabric even with the seam allowance.

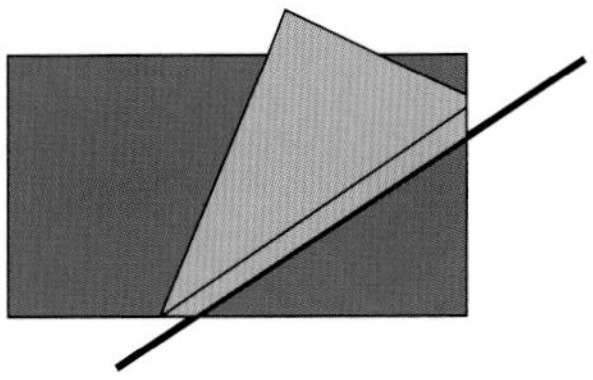

Trimming the excess

5. Repeat for the other side, once again varying the area that the triangle covers.

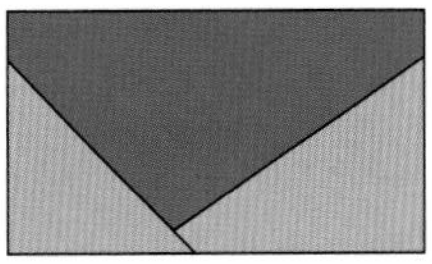

One happy goosez unit

Now moving on down the path with the two goosez in one...

DOUBLE FLYING GOOSEZ UNIT

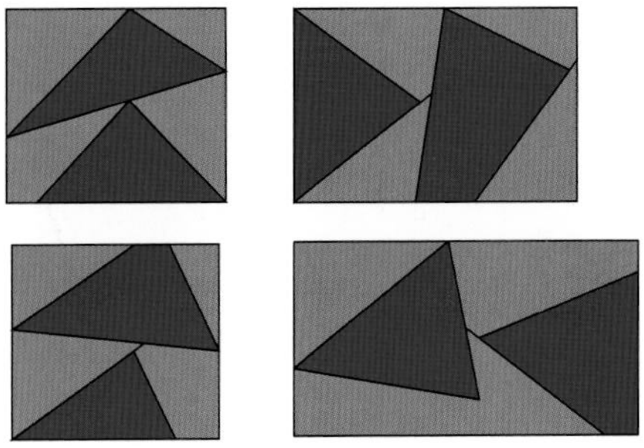

This is where we can start to get really nice and crooked...

Cutting Recipe for Double Flying Goosez Unit

1. Decide on the finished size of the unit.

2. Add 1/4" all around.

3. Add another 1/2" to the side to be sliced, as shown in the example on page 38. Cut the goosez fabric to this measurement.

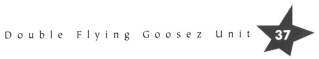

4. Cut two squares the finished length of the goosez piece from background fabric. Slice them in half-ish from corner to corner.

An Example

1. I need a 6" finished square.

2. I add ¼" all around, which brings it to 6½" square.

3. I add ½" as shown. I cut the goosez fabric 6½" x 7".

*Adding the
seam allowance*

4. I cut two 6"-ish squares from background fabric and slice them in half-ish from corner to corner.

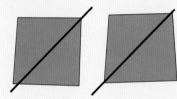

*Adding ½"
per slice*

Slicing into triangles

Piecing a Double Flying Goosez Unit

1. Place the goosez piece right side up and make a crooked slice along the length that you have allowed for. Separate these slightly.

2. Place the first background triangle for the first goosez piece in the desired position, also right side up. I generally vary its position from unit to unit: some starting left, on, or right of center, some over, some on, and some under the corner.

Trying out the triangle

3. Flip the triangle over so the pieces are right sides together, at the same time pulling it a little toward the corner to account for the seam allowance. Stitch.

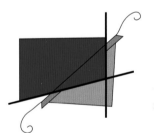

Flipped and stitched

4. With the right sides down, trim the triangle edges even with the goosez piece.

*Trimming even with
the goosez piece*

5. Flip the unit over, pull back the triangle, and trim the excess background fabric even with the seam allowance.

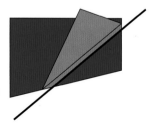

Trimming the excess

6. Repeat with the other side, then the other goosez piece, once again varying the area that the triangle covers.

First goose complete

7. Stitch the two goosez back together along their initial cut.

Two goosez make a double

And we continue now with flocks of flying goosez in a...

MULTIPLE FLYING GOOSEZ UNIT

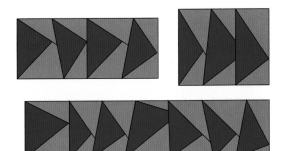

These are great as borders and edgings. They can even change flight direction mid-block!

Cutting Recipe for a Multiple Flying Goosez Unit

1. Decide on the finished size of the unit.

2. Add ¼" all around.

3. Add another ½" for each slice. Cut the goosez fabric to this measurement.

4. Cut a background square for each of the goosez equal to the finished length of a goosez piece. Slice them in half-ish from corner to corner.

An Example

1. I need a unit that is 4" x 8" finished.

2. I add ¼" all around, which brings it to 4½" x 8½".

Adding the seam allowance

3. I want four goosez in this unit and allow ½" as shown for each of the three slices needed. I cut a piece of goosez fabric 4½" x 10".

Adding ½" per slice

4. I cut four 4"-ish squares from background fabric and slice them in half-ish from corner to corner.

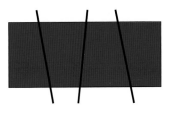

Slicing into triangles

Piecing a Multiple Flying Goosez Unit

1. Place the goosez piece right side up, and slice it in crooked, but equal-ish, pieces along the length that you have allowed for. Separate these slightly.

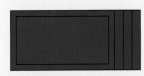

Slicing the goosez piece

2. Place the first background triangle right side up for the first goosez piece in the position you desire. I generally vary its position from unit to unit, some starting left, on, or right of center, some over, some on, and some under the corner, being careful to make all of the goosez fly in the same direction.

Auditioning the triangle

3. Flip the triangle over so the pieces are right sides together, at the same time pulling it toward the corner a little to allow for the seam allowance. Stitch and press.

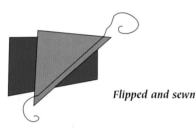

Flipped and sewn

4. With the right sides down, trim the triangle edges even with the goosez piece.

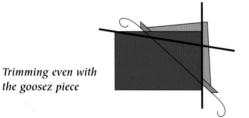

Trimming even with the goosez piece

5. Flip the unit over, pull back the triangle, and trim the excess background fabric even with the seam allowance.

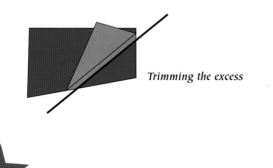

Trimming the excess

6. Repeat with the other side, then with all the other goosez pieces, once again varying the area that the triangles cover.

A lonely goosez unit

7. Stitch the goosez back together along their initial slices.

Finished goosez all in a row

Let's leave the goosez to go their own way and I'll show you how to cover a rectangle...

COVER CORNER RECTANGLEZ UNIT

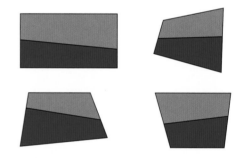

Yes, I know that rectangles shouldn't really be in this section, but the technique is the same as for triangles, and will help you make great blocks like Churn Dashez later. These Two-Patchez units can be used as an odd-shaped part of a sliced block. Stick with the Two-Patchez unit if you are making a "proper" rectangle.

Cutting Recipe for a Cover Corner Rectanglez Unit

1. Lay the background piece to be covered on your table.

2. Cut a rectangle from another fabric half the bigger width plus 1"-ish and cut the length plus 1"-ish more than the background.

An Example

1. My background piece is approximately 2" x 3" x 6".

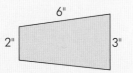

Background piece

2. I cut a rectangle 2½"-ish by 7"-ish.

Rectangle piece

Piecing a Cover Corner Rectanglez Unit

1. With the background piece right side up, place the rectangle piece in the desired position, also right side up. I generally vary its position from unit to unit: some aiming right, some left, some thick and some thin.

Testing the look

2. Flip the rectangle over so the pieces are right sides together, at the same time pulling it toward the edge to be covered to allow for the seam allowance. Stitch.

Sewing the pieces

3. With the right sides down, trim the edges of the rectangles pieces even with the background piece.

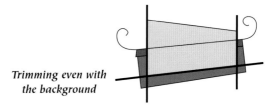

Trimming even with the background

4. Flip the unit over, pull back the rectangle, and trim the excess background fabric even with the seam allowance.

Trimming the excess

5. Your unit is complete.

A cover corner rectangle complete

EXTENDING THE TRIANGLEZ OPTIONS

In the previous recipes, our Double and Multiple Flying Goosez Units have the same fabric throughout because they have been cut from a single piece. To vary that look, cut more than one goosez piece. Lay them stacked exactly on top of each other with all right sides facing up. Slice them into crooked goosez and place them on the cutting mat in their original positions. Now switch goosez pieces between the different rows but maintain the same position. This will make multiple units; for example, a stack of four goosez pieces will make four same-style goosez units.

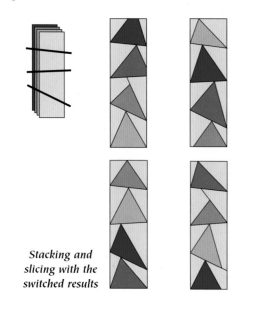

Stacking and slicing with the switched results

The background squares/triangles can also be cut from a multitude of fabrics and paired or assorted for a deliciously scrappy look. All the corner triangles can be made bigger or smaller to suit the look you want. You may want the corners/backgrounds sparse, so just change the recipe and make the background squares a little smaller. You may want all the corners/backgrounds prominent or overlapping; for these just cut the background squares a little larger.

In the Double and Multiple Flying Goosez Units, you may choose to reverse the directions of some goosez for a different effect.

Confused goosez

You may want your triangles to extend a little further, to be a little spikier. If so, cut the Cover Corner Trianglez fabric a little longer—as a rectangle rather than a square—then slice it in half-ish from corner to corner. If you want the spikes working in both directions you must cut two rectangles and slice them up, one right and one left.

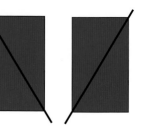

Cutting spikier triangles

Making Broken Dishez Like Mine

Broken Dishez by Jan Mullen, 44^{1}/$_{2}$" x 56^{1}/$_{2}$", 1999.

UNITS/TECHNIQUES USED

Cover Corner Trianglez Units

Four units join to make a Broken Dishez block.

Refer to the cutting and piecing instructions for Cover Corner Trianglez units on page 34.

COLOR STORY

Over the years I have collected an array of bright feature prints; I felt this was the right time to use them. The Broken Dishez pattern relies on two contrasting fabrics per block, so I simply paired up pleasing prints, trying not to let any print dominate. When all the blocks were made, I created some order by setting them in diagonal runs of color. This type of order is a great way to unite diverse blocks. You will see runs of yellow and green running diagonally from left to right. I felt the border needed to tie these busy blocks together, and I think the green fabrics helped. Unity was achieved by using green for the backgrounds of all the units and facing the colored corners toward the quilt

body. Finishing the top this way then made it a "green" quilt, which "let" the other colors contrast. Combining the fabrics in a different way will change the mood of the quilt.

Quilt Size: 44$\frac{1}{2}$" x 56$\frac{1}{2}$"

Block Size and Set: Blocks are 6" square, set six by eight for a total of forty-eight blocks. Each block is made up of four 3" square Cover Corner Trianglez Units.

FABRIC REQUIREMENTS

Focus Fabrics = 2 yards of assorted prints

Backgrounds = 2 yards of assorted prints

Inner Border = $\frac{1}{4}$ yard blue

Outer Border Focus Fabrics = $\frac{3}{4}$ yard of assorted prints

Outer Border Backgrounds = $\frac{3}{4}$ yard of assorted green prints

CUTTING & PIECING THE QUILT BODY

I chose forty-eight pairs of fabrics and cut a block each from these pairings.

For Each Block Cut

3$\frac{1}{2}$" **squares:** two focus fabrics and two background.

4$\frac{1}{2}$"-**ish squares:** one focus fabric and one background. Slice these squares in half-ish from

corner to corner to make four triangles.

Piece four sets of Cover Corner Trianglez units.

Arrange them with all the triangles facing in to the center, colors opposing. Sew the four units together to form a block.

Make the forty-eight blocks and arrange them in a pleasing way. Sew the blocks together to form the quilt body.

INNER BORDERS

Sides: Piece and cut two strips 1$\frac{1}{2}$" x 48$\frac{1}{2}$". Add to the quilt body.

Top and bottom: Cut two strips 1 $\frac{1}{2}$" x 38$\frac{1}{2}$". Add to the quilt body.

CUTTING AND PIECING THE OUTER BORDERS

We need two similar units in different sizes plus corner units to make the border fit the body.

Unit 1

Cut forty-eight 3$\frac{1}{2}$" green squares as backgrounds.

Cut twenty-four 4$\frac{1}{2}$"-ish colored squares. Slice these in half-ish from corner to corner.

Make forty-eight Cover Corner Trianglez units for the sides, top, and bottom.

Unit 2

Cut eight 3½" x 4½" rectangles from different greens.

Cut four 4½"-ish colored squares. Slice them in half-ish from corner to corner.

Sew a colored triangle onto one corner of each green rectangle, with four on left corners and four on right corners so the pattern continues around the corners. These eight Cover Corner Trianglez units are for the inner corners.

Unit 2, face half left and half right

Unit 3 Corners

Cut four 3½" green squares.

Arrange two sides with fourteen of Unit 1, with a Unit 2 at each end, keeping the Corner Trianglez units paired and facing in. Stitch to the quilt body.

Make a top and a bottom with ten of Unit 1, a Unit 2 at each inner end, and a Unit 3 at each end, once again keeping the Corner Trianglez units paired and facing in. Sew to the quilt body.

MACHINE QUILTING

Detail of Broken Dishez

Lots of interesting prints cried out for lots of interesting motifs. My usual stars, hearts, and daisies were featured, but I also used kisses, hugs, butterflies, suns, and leaves. I quilted what I thought of as background fabrics—most of these were greens and yellows. These are diagonal runs of color working from the top left to the bottom right of each block, tying the fabrics together.

Starz and Stripez by Jan Mullen, 35¹/₂" x 43", 1999.

UNITS/TECHNIQUES USED

Melon Patchez units, four corners covered

Melon Patchez units, two corners covered

Refer to the cutting and piecing instructions for Melon Patchez units on page 35.

You will cover four corners of some melons and only two corners of others.

COLOR STORY

This quilt pattern can make a feature of the lattice, the backgrounds, or the stars. I wanted to feature only the stars, so I decided to use a variety of pretty blues for the background squares and the lattice rectangles so they melded together as one surface for the stars to float on. A variety of rich reds for the star points made these stand out sufficiently.

I almost put an assortment of colors in the center of the stars but decided to keep it rather plain by using a set of black and white prints. This is a comparatively gentle color scheme and would look great in a nursery.

Quilt Size: 35½" x 43"

Block Size and Set: This quilt is made in an overall repeat pattern of different-sized units rather than traditional blocks. The Melon Patchez units are 2½" x 5", the large blue background square is 5", and the black and white center squares are 2½". Set the stars four by five.

FABRIC REQUIREMENTS

Background Squares = 1 yard of assorted blues

Background Lattice = ³⁄₄ yard of assorted blues

Star Centers = ¹⁄₄ yard of assorted black/white prints

Star Points = 1 yard of assorted reds

UNIT CUTTING AND PIECING

Unit 1

Cut twenty 3" squares for the star centers.

Unit 2

Cut thirty 5½" squares for background squares.

Unit 3

Cut thirty-one 3" x 5½" rectangles for the background lattice.

Cut sixty-two 3½"-ish squares for star points. Slice these in half-ish from corner to corner.

Make Melon Patch units with four corners covered.

Unit 4

Cut eighteen 3" x 5½" rectangles for the background lattice.

Cut eighteen 3½"-ish squares for star points. Slice these in half-ish from corner to corner.

Make Melon Patch units with two corners covered.

PIECING THE TOP

Use the photo to help you arrange unit placement. Essentially, all Unit 4s are placed around the edge, star point facing in toward the quilt body. Arrange and sew rows together to form the top.

MACHINE QUILTING

Detail of Starz and Stripez

I tried to differentiate the lattice from the background slightly by quilting the lattice in double, slightly wavy lines and the background squares in a mix of curls and swirls. As the stars were the main feature they were left to shine alone.

Making Dutchman'z Puzzle Like Mine

Dutchman'z Puzzle by Jan Mullen, 45^1/$_2$" x 64^1/$_2$", 1999.

UNITS/TECHNIQUES USED

Double Flying Goosez units

Four units joined together to make a Dutchman'z Puzzle Block.

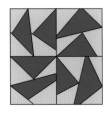

Multiple Flying Goosez unit on the border

Refer to the cutting recipe and piecing instructions for the Double Flying Goosez unit on page 37. For the border follow the cutting and piecing instructions for the Multiple Flying Goosez unit on page 39.

COLOR STORY

This time my ever-growing collection of yellows prompted the color scheme. A varied group of yellows is great for a subtly interesting, stable, light, and happy background. Color groups of hot pink, red, green, purple, and blue were each kept contained within blocks to highlight the difference in color. The black and white block borders served to not only separate the goosez points, but also to cool down the richness of the yellows.

Quilt Size: 45½" x 64½"

Block Size and Set: The Dutchman'z Puzzle blocks are 8" square; with borders the finished block size is 9½", set four by six for a total of twenty-four blocks. The Double Flying Goosez unit is 4" square.

FABRIC REQUIREMENTS

Backgrounds = 2½ yards of assorted yellows

Goosez = 1¾ yards of assorted colors

Block Borders = 1½ yards of assorted black/whites

Border Backgrounds = 1¼ yards of assorted yellows

Border Goosez = 1 yard of assorted colors

CUTTING & PIECING THE BLOCKS

For each block I cut four similar goosez fabrics and worked from a basket of cut assorted background triangles.

For Each Block

Cut four 4½" x 5" rectangles from goosez fabric.

Cut eight 4"-ish squares from background fabrics. Slice them in half-ish from corner to corner.

Make each goosez rectangle into a Double Flying Goosez unit.

Sew these four units together turning either clockwise or counter-clockwise.

Borders for Each Block

Sides: Cut two 2" x 8½" strips from black/white fabrics.

Top and bottom: Cut two 2" x 11½" strips from the same fabrics.

Sew these onto the block, and then square it to 10", placing the ruler slightly off center to skew the block.

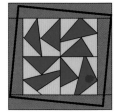

Squaring up the bordered block

Sew the twenty-four blocks together to form the quilt body.

OUTER BORDERS

Border Blocks

Cut twenty 4" x 12" rectangles from goosez fabrics. Stack them in four sets of five colors. I made one stack each of red, pink, blue, and purple. Slice each four times to make five goosez. Lay out and switch the pieces within the color groups.

Cut one hundred 3½"-ish squares from background fabrics. Slice these in half-ish from corner to corner.

Make twenty Multiple Flying Goosez units. These are finished at 3½" x 9½".

Corner Units

Cut four 4" squares from goosez fabrics.

Cut four 4"-ish squares from background fabrics. Slice them in half-ish from corner to corner.

Cut four 2½" x 5"-ish rectangles from background fabrics.

Sew the two triangles onto the goosez squares as for the Single Flying Goosez units (page 36). Complete the corner units by covering with the Cover Corner Rectanglez unit (page 40) to complete and float the goosez.

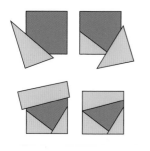

Sewing and trimming the corner units

Piece the six border units together for the side borders.

Sew to the quilt body.

Piece four border units together for the top and bottom borders and add the corner units to each end. Sew to the quilt body.

MACHINE QUILTING

Detail of Dutchman'z Puzzle

Because these goosez are flying wildly I felt that the quilting motifs should be looking sky-wards. Hence we have the usual free stars now joined by clouds, lightning strikes, birds, and hail stones. All these are stitched in the background yellows to push the goosez forward.

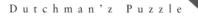

CHAPTER 5

Mainly Logz

Hands up those who haven't made a Log Cabin. It's an easy block that can be made in many ways with numerous variations. I've looked at it three different ways: the usual four-sided Log Cabin, odd-shaped logs reminiscent of the beautiful pineapple blocks, and a series of Squares-in-Squares units, which could sit just as well in the rectangles or triangles chapters, but which suited the theme of building up and cutting down.

You will be making heaps of decisions as you cut and sew because the recipes are minimal.

In this chapter please remember:

- All trimming is done in straight lines with a rotary cutter and ruler.

- Sewing should be done with a $1/4$"-ish seam, but a straight seam is more important.

- All these blocks can be made as a square or a rectangle. The Squarez-in-Squarez blocks would need a name change, though!

- When working out the math of a unit in these recipes, round up the measurement to the nearest half-inch.

- The strips in these blocks can be cut tapered or straight. For example, a tapered 2"-ish strip may vary from 1" at one end of the strip to $2^{1}/2$" at the other. It may also be a straight 2" strip. The recipes will be worked out "straight," but I give you permission to taper—I do it!

- The length of the strip is arbitrary. Generally, I find it best to cut on the lengthwise grain and trim the strips to the correct length as I use them. As I often cut from $1/2$ yard pieces, my strips are cut that length (about 18").

- I cut a pile of strips and place them in color baskets, topping them up when I run out of my favorites. This makes it easier to blend colors at the machine and work quickly.

We start this chapter with the...

LOG CABINZ UNIT

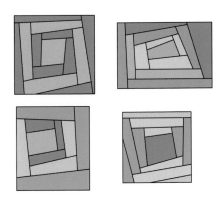

Usually a Log Cabin is built around the central square with strips added in clockwise order. Here we start with a crooked square and add to it with crooked strips. If we trim as we go and then square up at the end of each round, the block shape is kept manageable and perfectly accurate. No need for tedious foundations!

Cutting Recipe for a Log Cabinz Unit

1. Decide on the finished size of the unit.

2. Determine the approximate size of the center square. Add 1/4" all around.

3. Measure between the center square and the final edge of the block. Decide how many logs you will need to fill this space. Divide the log space by the number of logs you need to find the average width of the strips.

4. Add 1" to that average width to equal the approximate size of the strips to be cut.

An Example

12" square

1. I need a 12" finished square.

2. I want a center square finished 3"-ish. I cut the center square 3 1/2"-ish.

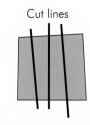

Sizing an odd-shaped center square

3. I have approximately 4 1/2" left to fill around the center square. I want about four strips; they need to be about 1"-ish wide.

4. I cut my strips 2"-ish wide.

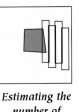

Cut lines

Estimating the number of logs needed

Cutting tapered logs

Piecing a Log Cabinz Unit

1. Sew the first strip onto the center square. Trim the lower edge of the strip along the bottom of the center square, shaping the center at the same time.

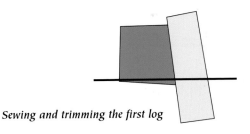

Sewing and trimming the first log

2. Rotate the center square counter-clockwise. Add the second strip, starting from the top edge of the first strip. Trim the lower edge of the strip along the bottom of the center square, shaping the center at the same time.

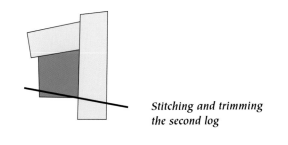

Stitching and trimming the second log

3. Add the next two strips following the same steps.

4. Assess the shape and size of your block. Trim as desired to make it straighter or more crooked.

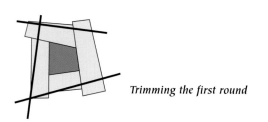

Trimming the first round

5. Continue with as many rounds as needed to make the block the required size. You may find that you need only one, two, or three strips in the final round to get it to block size. Add strips as necessary.

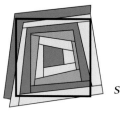

There is still space to fill in the left corner

6. Trim the edges to the unfinished block size.

Squaring up

If we change the shape of the center from a "square" to another shape—it can be three-, five-, six-sided or more—the look of the block varies greatly. Let me introduce you to my...

ODD-SHAPED LOG CABINZ UNIT

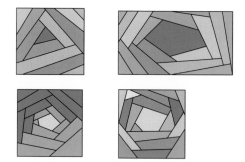

I like the way spherical qualities can be achieved using additional strips. Doesn't the eye do a beautiful job blending for us?

Cutting Recipe for an Odd-Shaped Log Cabinz Unit

1. Decide on the finished size of the unit.

2. Determine the approximate size of the center square. Add $1/4$" all around before you cut.

3. Measure between the center square and the block edge. Decide how many logs you need to fill this space. Divide the log space by the number of logs you need to find the average width of the strips.

4. Add 1" to that average width for the approximate width of the strips.

An Example

1. I need a 9" finished square.

2. I want a center square $1\frac{1}{2}$"-ish across, so I cut a 2"-ish square.

Sizing the center square

3. I have approximately 4" left around the center square to fill. I want about four strips, each about 1"-ish wide.

Finding the log size

Cut lines

4. I cut my strips 2"-ish wide.

Cutting tapered logs

Piecing an Odd-Shaped Log Cabinz Unit

1. Trim the center square to the desired shape.

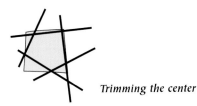

Trimming the center

2. Sew the first strip onto the center shape. Trim the lower edge of the strip equal to the bottom of the center shape.

*First log stitched
and trimmed*

3. Rotate the center shape counter-clockwise. Add the second strip, starting from the top edge of the first strip. Trim the lower edge of the strip equal to the bottom of the center shape.

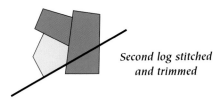

*Second log stitched
and trimmed*

4. Add the next strips in this round the same way. Assess the shape and size of your block. Trim as desired to make it straighter or more crooked. You may choose to create more or fewer sides as you go; for example, it is easy to start with five sides and finish with six.

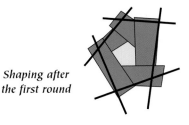

*Shaping after
the first round*

5. Continue adding strips until the block is the required size. You may find that you need only one, two, or three strips in the final round to make it the right size. Add what is necessary.

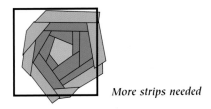

More strips needed

6. Trim the edges to the unfinished block size.

*Block ready for
squaring up*

Changing direction slightly, we will push the logs to the side of the path and work at building units that are a continual addition of triangles placed to look like squares. In these units we extend from a center square as before, but the subsequent squares are turned on point.

SQUAREZ-IN-SQUAREZ UNIT

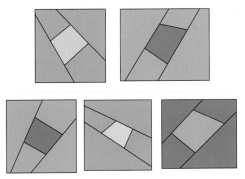

This recipe offers a unit with a floating center square. You can choose to follow the start of the Double Squarez-in-Squarez recipe (page 57) if you prefer the centers closer to the edge.

Cutting Recipe for a Squarez-in-Squarez Unit

1. Decide on the finished size of the unit.

2. Measure the corner-to-corner length of your unit (you can do this on your cutting mat) and round up the measurement to the nearest inch.

3. Divide this measurement by three to get the center square measurement.

4. Add $1/4$" all around the center square measurement to equal the cutting size of the center square and its two adjacent background pieces.

5. Double the center square measurement, add $1/4$" all around, and cut a background square this size. Slice it in half-ish from corner to corner to make the background triangles.

An Example

1. I need an 8" finished square.

2. The corner-to-corner length is over 11" (call it 12").

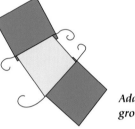

Measuring corner-to-corner length

3. This 12", divided by three, makes the center square measurement equal 4".

Center square measurement

4. I add $1/4$" all around this center square measurement and cut the center square and two adjacent backgrounds $4^1/2$"-ish square.

5. I double the center square measurement to make 8", and add $1/4$" all around. I cut the background square $8^1/2$"-ish, which I then slice in half-ish from corner to corner to make the background triangles.

Cutting the center and background squares   *Slicing the background triangles*

PIECING A SQUAREZ-IN-SQUAREZ UNIT

1. Trim the center square to the desired shape.

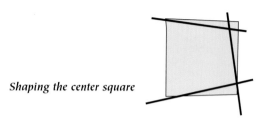

Shaping the center square

2. Sew the background squares to opposite sides of the center square.

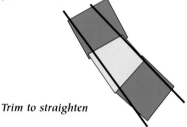

Adding the background squares

3. Trim both lengthwise sides to straighten the edges and reshape.

Trim to straighten

4. Add the background triangles to build the block up to a square. If you sew with the triangle underneath, the bias won't stretch as much!

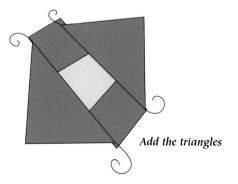

Add the triangles

5. Trim the block to the unfinished size.

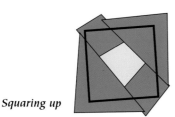

Squaring up

Moving on quickly in this direction we approach the...

DOUBLE SQUAREZ-IN-SQUAREZ UNIT

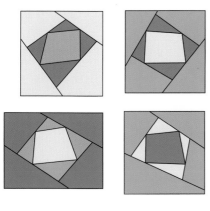

This is also designed so the two center squares seem to float within the edges for a strong graphic look.

Cutting Recipe for a Double Squarez-in-Squarez Unit

1. Decide on the finished size of the unit.

2. Measure the corner-to-corner length of your unit (you can do this on your cutting mat), and round up the measurement to the nearest inch.

3. Divide this measurement by three, rounding up to the nearest $1/2$" to get the center square measurement. Cut a center square this size.

4. Add $1/4$" all around to the center square measurement and cut two squares. Slice them in half-ish from corner to corner. These triangles make up the middle square.

5. Double the center square measurement and cut two squares on the lean side of this measure. Slice them in half-ish from corner to corner. These triangles make up the outer edge.

An Example

1. I need a 9" finished square.

2. The corner-to-corner length is more than 12" (call it 13").

3. This 13" divided by three means the center square measurement rounds up to $4^{1}/_{2}$". I cut a $4^{1}/_{2}$"-ish center square.

4. I add $1/4$" all around the center square measurement and then cut two 5"-ish squares. I slice them in half-ish from corner to corner. These triangles are used to complete my middle square.

5. I double the center square measurement to equal 9" and cut two squares on the lean side of this measure, between 8" and 9"-ish square. These are sliced in half-ish from corner to corner for the outer square triangles.

Measuring the corner-to-corner length

Cutting a center square

Slice the squares into triangles

Slice the outer squares into triangles

Piecing a Double Squarez-in-Squarez Unit

1. Trim the center square to the desired shape.

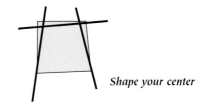

Shape your center

2. Sew two middle square triangles to opposite sides of the center square.

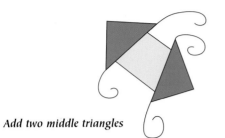

Add two middle triangles

3. Trim the side lengths to straighten the edges.

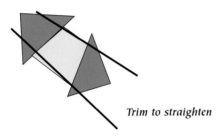

Trim to straighten

4. Add the last two opposing middle square triangles.

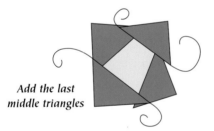

Add the last middle triangles

5. Using your ruler to guide you, trim ¼" from the center square points on each side, straightening and reshaping at the same time.

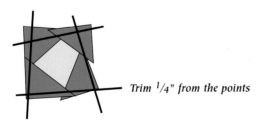

Trim ¹/₄" from the points

6. Sew two outer square triangles to opposite sides.

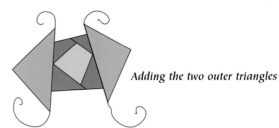

Adding the two outer triangles

7. Trim the side lengths to straighten the edges.

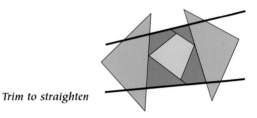

Trim to straighten

8. Sew on the last two outer edge triangles.

Add the last triangles

9. Trim to the unfinished block size.

Square up the block

The end of this particular pathway concludes with a...

TRIPLE SQUAREZ-IN-SQUAREZ UNIT

I had a burning desire to include Snailz Trailz in my quilt selection, so the recipe to make a Triple Squarez-in-Squarez unit was necessary. Unlike the single and double versions, this time the points of the last center square were designed to be close to the edge so that, when joined together, a group of these units meld together with only the occasional interruption.

Cutting Recipe for a Triple Squarez-in-Squarez Unit

1. Decide on the finished size of the unit.

2. Measure the corner-to-corner length of your unit (you can do this on your cutting mat), and round up the measurement to the nearest inch.

3. Divide this measurement by four, rounding up to the nearest $1/2$" to get the center square measurement.

4. Add $1/4$" all around and cut a center square to this size.

5. Using this cut size, cut two more squares. Slice them in half-ish from corner to corner. These triangles make up the second square.

6. Multiply the center square measurement one-and-a-half times, round that number up to the nearest $1/2$", and cut two squares this size. Slice them in half-ish from corner to corner. These triangles make up the third square.

7. Double the center square measurement from step 4. Cut two squares to this size. Slice them in half-ish from corner to corner. These triangles make up the outer edge.

An Example

1. I need a 6" finished square.

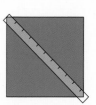

Measuring the corner-to-corner length

2. The corner-to-corner length is more than 8".

3. I divide the 9" measurement by four, which equals $2 1/4$". Then I round this number up so the center square measurement equals $2 1/2$".

Determining the center square measurement

4. I add $1/4$" all around and cut a center square 3"-ish.

5. I use this cut size again and cut two more 3"-ish squares. I slice them in half-ish from corner to corner. These triangles are used for the second round.

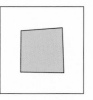

Cutting the center square

6. I multiply the original center square measurement of $2 1/2$" one-and-a-half-times (to $3 3/4$), and round it up to 4". I cut two 4"-ish squares, and slice them in half-ish from corner to corner. These triangles are added for the third round.

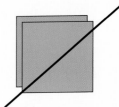

Slicing squares for second round triangles

7. Finally, I double the center square measurement. I cut two 5"-ish squares, then slice them in half-ish from corner to corner. These triangles are used for the outer edge.

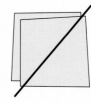

Stacking and slicing squares for third round triangles

Stacking and slicing outer square triangles

Piecing a Triple Squarez-in-Squarez Unit

1. Trim the center square to the desired shape.

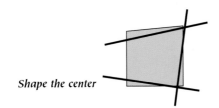

Shape the center

2. Sew two second round triangles to opposite sides of the center square.

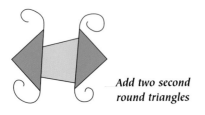

Add two second round triangles

3. Trim the side lengths to straighten the edges.

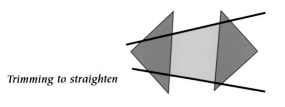

Trimming to straighten

4. Add the last two second round triangles.

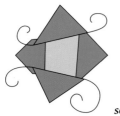

Add the other two second round triangles

5. Using your ruler, trim ¹/₄" from the center square points on each side, straightening and reshaping at the same time.

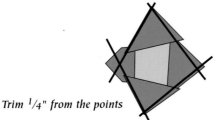

Trim ¹/₄" from the points

6. Add the next two sets of triangles in similar fashion.

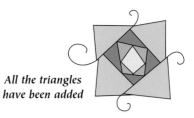

All the triangles have been added

7. Trim to the unfinished block size.

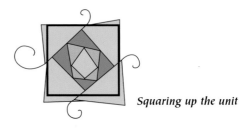

Squaring up the unit

EXTENDING THE LOGZ OPTIONS

You can achieve lots of variations when working with Log Cabinz blocks. You can add strips in different orders. For example, the traditional Courthouse Steps block has the first and second strips placed opposite each other, and continues the opposite placement rhythm.

Courthouse Stepz

Varying the color placement gives different effects. For example, rounds of a single color or totally random color placement in the blocks can take Log Cabinz blocks on different paths.

Bullseye Log Cabinz

Or you may choose to use these crooked blocks within one of many traditional Log Cabin settings. Two light sides and two dark sides offer infinite arrangements.

*Log Cabinz block
with traditional
lights and darks*

Strips can vary in width and length, and they can be joined from smaller lengths for a scrappier, more interesting and colorful effect.

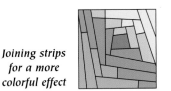

*Joining strips
for a more
colorful effect*

The center squares can be pieced units. For example, Roman Stripes, Four-Patchez, and Double Flying Goosez would all add interest to a Log Cabinz or Double Squarez-in-Squarez block.

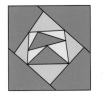

*Double Goosez in
Double Squarez*

You can start off with four-sided Log Cabinz units and then trim them to finish the blocks in an Odd-Shaped Logs style.

*Odd-shaped logs with
four-sided center*

Another option is to begin by making an Odd-Shaped Logz and end with four-sided Log Cabinz units.

*Log Cabinz with
odd log centers*

Or, you can make the Log Cabinz unit, realign it to diamond placement, and add on to the block size by adding corner strips.

Diamond logs

The center square can be off-center. It may even be so far up in a corner that it only has strips added on two sides!

Logs poked in a corner

You can wander around in Log Cabinz Land for years!

Making Log Cabinz Like Mine

Log Cabinz by Jan Mullen, 44¹/₂" x 64", 1999.

UNITS/TECHNIQUES USED

Log Cabinz units

Refer to the cutting and piecing instructions for Log Cabinz units on page 53.

COLOR STORY

I wanted to venture in a more nontraditional direction with this quilt. I decided to use multiple color choices rather than the usual lights and darks often found in regular Log Cabin quilts. The lights and darks are still there, but by using seven groups of color I could mix it all up and make the look less ordered. I used four different color groups per block, with a center feature fabric bordered in a strong first round of black logs as a striking focus. The border and binding are the centers in reverse.

Quilt Size: 44 1/2" x 64"

Block Size and Set: Blocks are 10", set four by six for a total of twenty-four blocks.

FABRIC REQUIREMENTS

Center Squares = a fat quarter of a feature print

First Round Logs = 1/2 yard black

Logs = 5 yards of assorted colors; 1/2 yard, fat quarters, or fat-eighth cuts will give you best use of grain and length

Border = 1/2 yard of black

CUTTING & PIECING THE BLOCKS

Centers

Cut twenty-four 3" squares.

Black Logs around Centers

Cut 1" to 1 1/2"-ish strips of black fabric on the lengthwise grain. Trim as needed.

Logs

Cut tapered 1" to 2 1/2"-ish strips on the lengthwise grain. Trim to size as needed. Use a variety of mixed colored fabrics. Cut a basketful of each color, start sewing, and cut more strips as you need them.

Follow the piecing instructions for the Log Cabinz units on page 53.

Make the blocks at least 10 1/2" all around before squaring to this unfinished size.

Arrange the blocks and sew them together to form the quilt body.

BORDERS

Sides: Piece and cut two strips 2 1/2" x 60 1/2". Add to the quilt body.

Top and bottom: Piece and cut two strips 2 1/2" x 44 1/2". Sew onto the quilt body.

MACHINE QUILTING

Detail of Log Cabinz

I am particularly pleased with the quilting here. I have always found it a challenge to come up with a quilting design for Log Cabinz quilts that not only didn't take away from the design, but which allowed some freedom and creativity—something that added to the top, not detracted from it! With this quilt I went organic and with double-stitched lines made a variety of curvy, crooked, loopy, wavy, zig-zaggy, leafy, and weavy lines. First I stitched around the centers, the first-round edges and the color sections of each block to stabilize them. Then it was pure double-stitching fun!

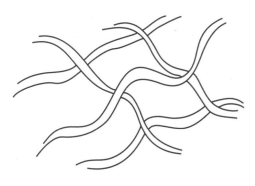

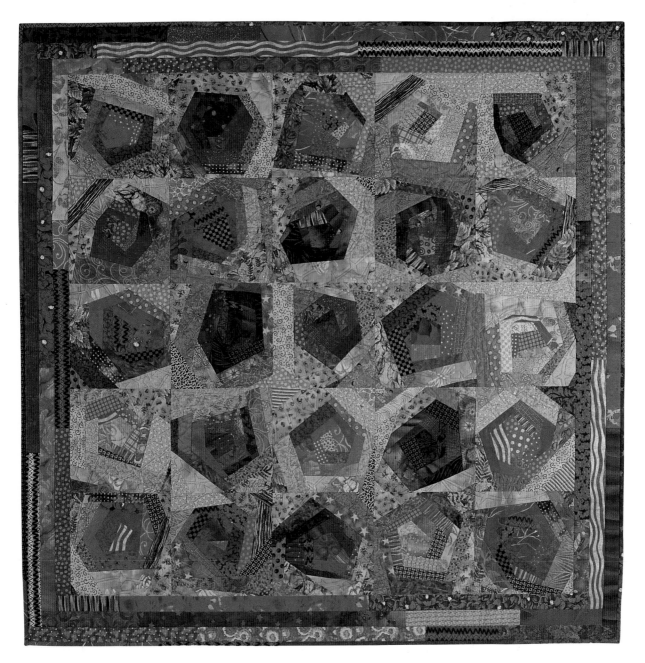

Log Flowerz by Jan Mullen, 48" square, 1999.

UNITS/TECHNIQUES USED

Odd-Shaped Log Cabinz Units

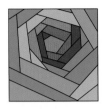

Refer to the cutting and piecing instructions for the Odd-Shaped Log Cabinz unit on page 54.

COLOR STORY

I've had Log Cabinz roses on my mind for years, but rather than produce a pretty rosebud quilt, I've gone for a version that is bolder, with more modern graphic leanings complete with quilted thorns. A large variety of greens, reds, purples, and oranges creates depth and interest. The greens in particular varied greatly—I used anything that vaguely worked and found that some of my least favorite fabrics worked very effectively to build up textured interest.

Quilt Size: 48" square

Block Size and Set: Blocks are 8" square set five by five for a total of twenty-five blocks.

FABRIC REQUIREMENTS

Flowers = 1½ yards of assorted reds, oranges, and purples

Backgrounds = 3½ yards of assorted greens

Borders = 1 yard of assorted reds, oranges, and purples

CUTTING & PIECING THE QUILT BODY

Centers

Cut twenty-five 3"-ish squares. Trim them to four-, five-, or six-sided shapes.

Flowers

Cut tapered 1" to 2"-ish strips of flowers fabrics on the lengthwise grain. Trim as needed. Cut a few strips from each of your fabrics, then cut more as needed.

Background Logs

Cut tapered 1" to 3"-ish strips on the lengthwise grain. Trim as needed. Cut a few strips from each of your fabrics, then cut more as needed.

Follow the basic piecing instructions for the Odd-Shaped Log Cabinz units (page 54), with these variations:

Add three rounds of the flower logs, trimming and reshaping as you finish each row. Complete the blocks with green strips. Make the blocks at least 8½" all around before squaring to this unfinished size. Arrange the blocks and sew together to form the quilt body.

BORDER

Cut 1¾"-ish wide strips of flowers fabrics. Arrange and sew them together to form rounds of a large Courthouse Steps border.

Round 1—Sides: two 40½" strips; **top and bottom**: two 43" strips.

Round 2—Sides: two 43" strips; **top and bottom**: two 45½" strips.

Round 3—Sides: two 45½" strips; **top and bottom**: two 48" strips.

MACHINE QUILTING

Detail of Log Flowerz

There were only two ways to go here; choose to pad this garden with leaves or line it with prickly thorns. I chose to go the hard, hurty way and loved the results of intertwined stylized branches. The flowers were quilted with wavy double spirals to hold them down and focus their centers.

Making Squarez-in-Squarez Like Mine

Squarez-in-Squarez by Jan Mullen, 41^1/$_2$" x 53^1/$_2$", 1999.

UNITS/TECHNIQUES USED

Squarez-in-Squarez Units

Refer to the cutting and piecing instructions for Squarez-in-Squarez units on page 55.

COLOR STORY

I found a beautiful marbled fabric that I loved, but I only had a little bit of it as the starting point for this quilt. I needed to add a lot of other fabrics, but wanted to let this fabric sing. I added purples, blue/greens, greens, and pinks for backgrounds and shining forth from the centers were some of these fabrics, plus some odd choice reds. Bold stripes in many of the centers added a lot of movement. The purple "spot" fabric also helped to create interest in the backgrounds. I feel that these squares float, dance, and sing all at the same time!

Quilt Size: 41½" x 53½"

Block Size and Set: Blocks are 6" set six by eight for a total of forty-eight blocks.

FABRIC REQUIREMENTS

Centers = ⅝ yard of assorted colors

Backgrounds = 3 yards of assorted colors

Borders = 1 yard of assorted colors

CUTTING & PIECING THE QUILT BODY

Centers

Cut forty-eight 3½" squares for the centers.

Backgrounds

For each center square you need two 3½"-ish squares and one 6½"-ish square, which is then sliced in half-ish from corner to corner.

Follow the piecing instructions for the Squarez-in-Squarez units on page 55. Trim each block to 6½" square.

Arrange the blocks and sew together to form the quilt body.

BORDER

Cut four 3" squares for the corners.

Cut eighty-four 3" x 3½"-ish rectangles. Sew them together in sets of three, varying the angles as you stitch so they are skewed. Trim each set to a 3" x 6½" unit. You should have twenty-eight of these.

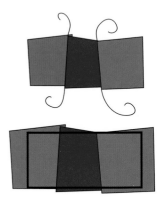

Sew and trim the border units

Sides: Piece eight units together. Sew to the quilt body.

Top and bottom: Piece six units together, then add a corner unit to each end. Sew to the quilt body.

MACHINE QUILTING

Detail of Squarez-in-Squarez

Once again, I tried to soften the hard edges of this pattern with the quilting. With double-stitched, double-ended curls on each corner of the blocks, it reminds me of the rich, exotic look of Moroccan tiles.

CHAPTER 6

Mainly Curvez

No need to be worried about cutting and piecing curves. The way I approach making curves in my crooked style should change your mind very quickly about trying these. In essence, we start with larger-than-needed backgrounds and freehand cut curves with a rotary cutter. It's such a lot of fun—no rulers and total freedom!

We slice, perhaps swap pieces, maybe cover corners, or build up inserts. Then we restitch, and finally, we trim off the rough edges to be left with pristine blocks, with skewed curves inset.

In this chapter please remember:

- The background squares are cut as an "ish" measurement.

- Sewing should be done with a $\frac{1}{4}$"-ish seam, but an even, smooth seam is more important than a perfectly sized one.

- All of these blocks may be made as a square or a rectangle.

- As you prepare to ease and pin the curved edges, gently fan out the outer background piece over the inner piece so the raw edges of both pieces match exactly, and the stitching area lies flat and can be held well.

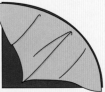

Stretching the cut background

- When pinning, don't let the point of the pin stray too far from the seam line.

- Practice freehand cutting on some scraps before attempting your first blocks. Be confident, cut carefully, and hold the stack in place well away from your blade!

Hands on cutters and off rulers, and let's set off with a...

DRUNKARD'Z PATH UNIT

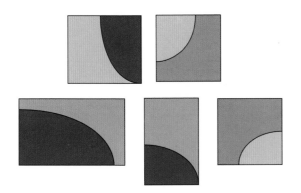

I've made these large, I've made them small, and I usually call them Tipsy blocks. I do love making them. You need to cut a stack of two fabrics to make these blocks quickly and easily. Try to vary the depth and shape of the curves from block to block. This method makes two blocks in positive and negative image. Stack and cut even more backgrounds for greater variations.

Cutting Recipe for a Drunkard'z Path Unit

1. Decide on the finished size of the unit.

2. Add $1/4$" all around.

3. Add a $3/4$" trimming allowance on two sides. Cut two backgrounds this size.

An Example

1. I need an 8" finished unit.

2. I add $1/4$" all around, which brings my background to $8\frac{1}{2}$" square.

3. I add the $3/4$" trimming allowance all around, which means I cut two 10"-ish squares.

Piecing a Drunkard'z Path Unit

1. Stack the two squares together on the cutting mat, right sides up.

Stack the backgrounds

2. Working freehand with a rotary cutter, cut a curve from one side to the adjacent side.

Freehand cut the curve

3. Switch the inner corners as you place them on your board.

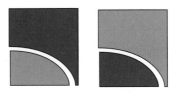

Switch the pieces

4. Mark the centers with chalk or a pencil.

Mark the centers

Place the pieces right sides together, and align and pin the centers on the seam line.

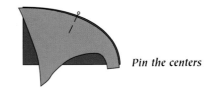

Pin the centers

Fan out the outer piece so the curved edges align. The inner piece will be approximately $1/2$" shorter on the outer edge. Pin these edges, then smooth the area between these two, pinning as you go on both sides.

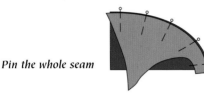

Pin the whole seam

5. Stitch the pieces with the outer piece face up on the machine, so you can ease out the folds while sewing.

Stitch

6. Trim to the unfinished unit size.

Squaring up the unit

Wasn't that one of the easiest things you've done? I think the only reason not to make thousands of them is that the pinning takes time, but it just has to be done to obtain an even spread of fabric. Onward, and now happily freehand cutting (I hope), we approach my...

GRANNIE'Z FAN UNIT

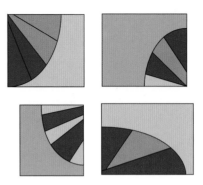

Grannie'z Fan takes Drunkard'z Path a step further. Only one background square is cut, and the inner corner is used as a foundation. If your fabric is precious, you can use your inner corner as a template for cutting a less important fabric. The inner corner is covered with wedges of fabric—how many and how big is up to you.

Cutting Recipe for a Grannie'z Fan Unit

1. Decide on the finished size of the unit.

2. Add $1/4$" all around.

3. Add a $3/4$" trimming allowance on two sides to give you the cutting size for the background square.

4. Decide on the width of the top edge of the wedges you would like in the inner corner. Add $1/2$" seam allowance on each side of the wedge to determine the width of the wedges. The length of these wedges can vary from the size of the block to any measurement that will cover the foundation. For single wedges, cut a rectangle the length and width you have decided on, then trim to shape before or after stitching to the foundation.

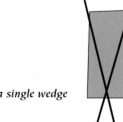

Cutting a single wedge

For pairs of wedges, cut rectangles the length and width you have decided on, then slice them in half-ish from corner to corner.

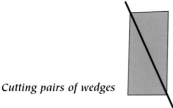

Cutting pairs of wedges

For multiple wedges, cut a strip as wide as the length of the wedges you need. Make the strip as long as is convenient for the number of wedges required. Slice up and down.

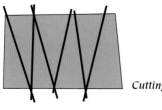

Cutting lots of wedges

An Example

1. I need a 12" finished unit.

2. I add 1/4" all around.

3. I add another 3/4" trimming allowance on two sides, so the background is cut 14"-ish square.

Adding the seam allowance

3/4"

Adding the trimming allowance

4. I want the wedges to come close to the center of the block, and these wedges require a maximum width of 3"-ish. I cut rectangles 4" x 12"-ish, then cut them in half-ish from corner to corner to make pairs of wedges.

Stack pairs of wedges for cutting

Piecing a Grannie'z Fan Unit

1. Lay the background square on the cutting mat right side up.

2. Working freehand with a rotary cutter, cut a curve from one side to the adjacent side.

Freehand cut the curve

3. Pick up the inner corner. Lay a wedge in the center of the inner corner that you are using as a foundation. Lay the second wedge on top of the first wedge, right sides together and raw edges aligned. Stitch.

Stitch the first two wedges together

4. Continue sewing on wedges, adding on in both directions, until the foundation is covered. Make sure the curved edge is covered; the side edges aren't so important. You may need to adjust alignment, and perhaps trim the width or shape of the wedges as you go, to achieve a nice balanced look.

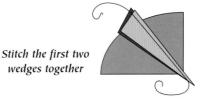

Fully wedged!

5. Trim the curved edge to its exact foundation shape. Trimming the side edges is not important.

Trimming the curved edge

6. Mark the centers with chalk or a pencil.

Mark the centers

Place the background and pieced fan pieces right sides together. Pin the centers on the seam line. Fan out the outer piece so the raw edges align comfortably with the corner curve and pin to 1/2"-ish from the side edges. Smooth the area between these two pins and pin between them on both sides.

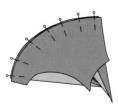

Pin the pieces together

7. Sew the pieces together with the background face up at the machine so you can ease out folds.

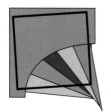

Sew together

8. Trim to the unfinished block size.

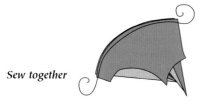

Squaring up the block

Finally, the last recipe (for now) on this crooked journey. I am very pleased with having produced...

WEDDING RING CORNERZ UNIT

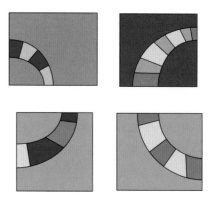

Confession time—I've never made a traditional Wedding Ring quilt! I like the look of them, but they always seemed like too much tedious, exacting work. Here I put the fun back into Wedding Rings by giving you my closely related version—Wedding Ring Cornerz. You will be pleasantly surprised at the ease with which they go together. You will enjoy making them so much that it may seem like you are on a continuous curvy honeymoon. Are you surprised to be in love with curves?

Cutting Recipe for a Wedding Ring Cornerz Unit

1. Decide on the finished size of the unit.

2. Add 1/4" all around.

3. Add a 1/2" trimming allowance all around to determine the cutting size of the background square.

4. Decide on the maximum height and width of your wedges and add 1/4" all around to determine your initial wedge size. It is easier and more economical to cut strips the height needed plus 1/2" and the length of the fabric you have, then slice these strips into crooked wedges.

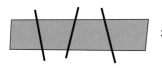

*Slicing strips
into wedges*

An Example

1. I need a 6" finished unit.

2. I add $1/4$" all around.

3. I add a $1/2$" trimming allowance on two sides, so I cut the background $7^{1}/2$"-ish square.

*Add the seam
allowance*

*Add the trimming
allowance*

4. I decide that the maximum height and width of the wedges should be 2", so I need to cut a $2^{1}/2$"-ish square. I decide to cut strips of varying lengths that are $2^{1}/2$" wide and slice these strips into crooked wedges for making more blocks later.

Stack cutting wedges

Piecing a Wedding Ring Cornerz Unit

1. Lay the background square on the cutting mat, right side up.

2. Sew the wedges together, varying the angles at which they are placed, until they are long enough to fill in the curve that you anticipate cutting. You may have to trim the wedges to a better shape as you go.

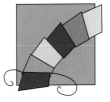

*Place the stitched wedges
on top of the background
square to check the size*

3. Freehand trim the inner and outer curves of the pieced wedges to a nice, even curve with a rotary cutter.

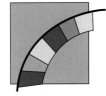

Freehand cut the curves

4. Place the pieced wedges against the background and, using the pieced wedges as a template, slice the background to match the outer curve.

*Cut the background
curve to echo the
curve of the wedges*

5. Trim the side edges of the pieced wedges to line up with the background sides.

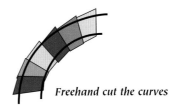

*Trimming the
wedge edges*

6. Mark the centers with a chalk wheel or a pencil. Place these pieces right sides together; align and pin the centers. Fan out the background piece so the raw edges align comfortably with the wedges' outer curve. Start pinning the wedges $1/2$"-ish from the background edges. Smooth the area between these two pins, then pin in between them on both sides.

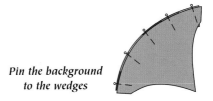

*Pin the background
to the wedges*

Sew the pieces with the background piece face up at the machine so you can ease out folds.

7. Trim the background corner to exactly echo the inner curve of the pieced wedges.

Trim the inner background to match the wedges

8. Mark the centers and pin as before, being careful not to stretch the stitching. You might want to stay-stitch this wedge edge to stabilize it. It is not necessary to keep the outer edges aligned. Stitch.

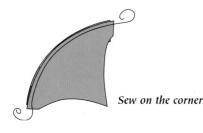

Sew on the corner

9. Trim to the unfinished block size.

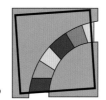

Squaring up

EXTENDING THE CURVEZ OPTIONS

Here are a few more ideas for curves. If you would like to make double Drunkard'z Path, Grannie'z Fanz, and Wedding Ring Corners within a single block, increase the size of the background blocks to account for the extra seam or seams.

Double Drunkard'z Path

You can cut into a pieced block. For example, one option is to pair a pieced Nine-Patchez unit with a plain background square, then stack, slice, switch, and sew. This creates a very unusual version of Drunkard'z Path.

Drunk Nine-Patchez

Another choice is to stack, slice, and switch backgrounds in the Wedding Ring Cornerz before adding the wedges. In this case you want to piece and trim the wedges to match the cut background curves rather than cutting the background curves to match the trimmed wedges.

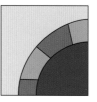

Switching corners

Finally, how about slicing a set of Drunkard'z Path blocks in half from corner to corner before their final trim, then stitching them to another half block? You could put lefts with rights to make Stepped Drunkard'z, or put rights to rights and lefts to lefts to make Flipped Drunkard'z!

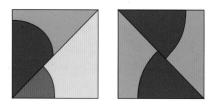

Stepped Drunkard'z and Flipped Drunkard'z

Making Drunkard'z Path Like Mine

Drunkard'z Path by Jan Mullen, 42¹/₂" x 58¹/₂", 1999.

UNITS/TECHNIQUES USED

Drunkard'z Path units

Four Drunkard'z Path units sewn together to make Honey Beez blocks.

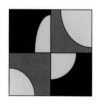

Refer to the cutting and piecing instructions for Drunkard'z Path units on page 71.

COLOR STORY

I have little obsessions about color combinations sometimes. My love of black and strong yellows seemed the right starting point for these blocks. The shape of the blocks also reminds me of busy bees—rounded bits of body and fluttering wings—so this color combination became even more applicable. The prints with bits of red, in particular, helped to move this quilt away from the potential flatness of using just two colors.

Quilt Size: 42½" x 58½"

Block Size and Set: Blocks are 8", set four by six for a total of twenty-four blocks. Each block is made up of four 4" Drunkard'z Path units.

FABRIC REQUIREMENTS

Blocks/Outer Pieced Border = 2¼ yards of assorted yellows and 2¼ yards of assorted blacks

Inner Border = ¼ yard of black

CUTTING & PIECING THE QUILT BODY

Cut ninety-six 6"-ish squares, forty-eight from blacks, forty-eight from yellows. Pair every black with an appropriate yellow and piece them according to the Drunkard'z Path instructions on page 71. Trim them to 4½" square.

Divide the units into those that have black backgrounds and those that have yellow backgrounds.

Sew together twelve sets of four units with black backgrounds. They need to be arranged with two yellow inner corners "kissing" and the opposing two yellow corners facing out.

Sew together twelve sets of four units with yellow backgrounds. They need to be arranged with two black inner corners "kissing"

and the opposing two black corners facing out.

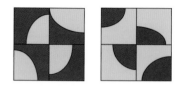

Black Honey Beez and yellow Honey Beez

Arrange the finished blocks in an alternating yellow and black background grid, to create a secondary pattern of the inner corners "kissing." Sew the blocks together to form the quilt body.

INNER BORDERS

Sides: Piece and cut two 1½" x 48½" strips.

Top and bottom: Piece and cut two 1½" x 42½" strips.

Cut four 1½" x 4½" filler strips to be used in the corners.

OUTER PIECED BORDERS

Cut forty-four 6"-ish squares—twenty-two from blacks, twenty-two from yellows. Pair every black with an appropriate yellow and piece them according to the Drunkard'z Path instructions. Trim them to 4½" square.

Sew together in pairs of same color backgrounds, with all inner corners "kissing."

For the corners, use two single black units and two single yellow units.

Sew two sets of six pairs together to form the side borders, alternating the background colors.

Sew two sets of four pairs together to form the top and bottom borders, alternating the background colors. Sew an inner border filler strip on each end of these, then complete with a single unit.

Add the inner border side strips, then the outer side borders.

Add the inner border strips, top and bottom, then the top and bottom outer borders.

Detail of Drunkard'z Path

Bee stings were on my mind here, I think, so every background—be it black or yellow—has spokes, rays, curls and other pointy bits extending from the curve.

Grannie'z Fanz by Jan Mullen, 47¹/₂" x 56¹/₂", 1999.

UNITS/TECHNIQUES USED

Grannie'z Fanz units

Refer to the cutting and piecing instructions for Grannie'z Fanz units on page 72.

COLOR STORY

Reds—bright, dull, dark, printed, and textured. These red backgrounds played host to ochres, teals, aquas, blacks, purples, and greens in an odd mix of textures and loud prints. The rather unusual combinations united the reds and the loud inner border.

Quilt Size: $47\frac{1}{2}$" x $56\frac{1}{2}$"

Block Size and Set: Blocks are 9", set four by five for a total of twenty blocks.

FABRIC REQUIREMENTS

Backgrounds = $2\frac{1}{4}$ yards of assorted reds

Block Wedges = $1\frac{1}{2}$ yards of assorted colors

Inner Border = $\frac{1}{4}$ yard of a colorful, dramatic print

Border Wedges = 2 yards of assorted colors

CUTTING & PIECING THE QUILT BODY

Cut twenty 11"-ish squares from background fabric.

Cut strips of wedge fabric 8"-ish wide and the length you desire. Cut into wedges with tops of $3\frac{1}{2}$"-ish, maximum. I used five wedges per block.

Make twenty blocks using the piecing instructions for Grannie'z Fanz on page 72.

Trim the blocks to $9\frac{1}{2}$" square.

Arrange the blocks and sew together to form the quilt body.

INNER BORDERS

Sides: Piece and cut two strips $1\frac{1}{2}$"x $45\frac{1}{2}$". Sew onto the quilt body.

Top and bottom borders: Cut two strips $1\frac{1}{2}$"x $38\frac{1}{2}$". Add to the quilt body.

OUTER BORDERS

Cut more wedge fabrics from $6\frac{1}{2}$"-ish wide strips of assorted colors. Cut them 3"-ish at the top and close to zero at the base. I used about 150 wedges.

From lightweight paper cut 5" strips and join with glue stick, if necessary, to make two sides, a top, and a bottom, each $47\frac{1}{2}$" long. Stitch the wedges onto this foundation paper, starting and stopping with backstitches, alternating wedge direction and

making sure that the paper is completely covered. If you shorten your stitch length it is easier to remove the paper.

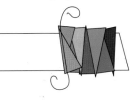

Sewing wedges onto the foundation

When the paper is covered with wedges, trim the rough edges back to the correct size, 5" x $47\frac{1}{2}$". Remove the paper. Add the side borders, then the top and bottom borders.

MACHINE QUILTING

Detail of Grannie'z Fanz

The quilting pattern here is very unlike what I usually do. I felt that the large expanses of background needed to be well filled, I wanted to accentuate the strong diagonal, and I didn't want anything too pointy—there are enough points on the wedges. What came about was something akin to a dinosaur backbone and is the biggest area of continuous quilting I've ever done!

Making Wedding Ringz Like Mine

Wedding Ringz by Jan Mullen, 52¹/₂" square, 1999.

UNITS/TECHNIQUES USED

Wedding Ring Cornerz units

Refer to cutting and piecing instructions for Wedding Ring Cornerz units on page 74.

COLOR STORY

I went for the blues this time, not exactly the ones I had in mind, but my fabric collection has a few gaps! I wanted a confetti-like effect, so I chose blues with prints—flowers, stars, spots, and cups. These prints are blurred by the eye and add interest to the large space behind the multicolored wedges in each block. Of course I couldn't contain myself to rings of a single color, so there are corners of aqua, red, yellow, green, pink and purple. Essentially they pick out the colors in the background prints.

Quilt Size: 52½" square

Block Size and Set: Blocks are 8", set six by six for a total of thirty-six blocks.

FABRIC REQUIREMENTS

Backgrounds = 2½ yards of assorted blue prints

Wedges = 1½ yards of assorted colors

CUTTING & PIECING THE QUILT BODY

Cut thirty-six 9½"-ish squares from background fabric.

Cut strips of wedge fabric 3½"-ish wide and the length you desire. I cut 9"-ish lengths from fifty-eight fabrics, which was enough to do the border as well. Cut into wedges with tops of 3"-ish and bases 2"-ish.

I used between four and seven wedges per block, which varied the look of each curve.

Make the blocks using the piecing instructions for Wedding Ring Cornerz units on page 74.

Trim the blocks to 8½" square.

Arrange the blocks and sew together to form the quilt body.

BORDERS

Using the leftover wedges, and cutting more as needed, sew together groups of eight wedges, this time sewing tops next to bottoms to make rectangles, not curves. Trim them to 2½" wide and square off their ends.

Trimming groups of border wedges

Sew enough of these border units together to make two sides 48½" long and a top and bottom each 52½" long. Add these borders to the quilt body.

MACHINE QUILTING

Detail of Wedding Ringz

Once again I had an expansive background to fill, but this time I wanted to add another dimension to the one-color background. Double-stitched waves, rays, zigzags, curls, and odd line variations accentuated the circles.

CHAPTER 7

Combining Techniques

We have worked through the basic units of crooked patchwork. The time is ripe to move on and take full advantage of what you have learned by combining two or more techniques in one block. In doing this you not only extend the range of blocks you can make, but you may also choose to combine techniques and come up with blocks of your own design.

Make sure your thinking caps are on when combining techniques. I find that to produce the look I desire, I sometimes need to modify a recipe. Each block may need special help so it still looks something like the traditional version. For example, trying to translate Pinwheels turned into a mini-challenge—it can look more like a Maltese Cross if you aren't on your toes! The solution there was quite simple—it was just a matter of making sure the appropriate corners were covered. The "extra crooked cutting allowance" often comes in handy, too; don't forget about its existence!

Please read through these next six patterns before launching out on your own. The instructions look more complicated than they really are, with my continual references to cutting and piecing instructions in the previous chapters. A quick read now may help to ward off some potential gremlins before you start wielding your rotary cutter. You'll probably find this chapter easier to approach if you have made the relevant sample units first, that is, those units that combine to make the featured blocks. It is wise to ALWAYS make a sample feature block as a matter of course.

Come on, I'm off, and I'm taking you with me!

Making Beggar Block
Butterfliez Like Mine

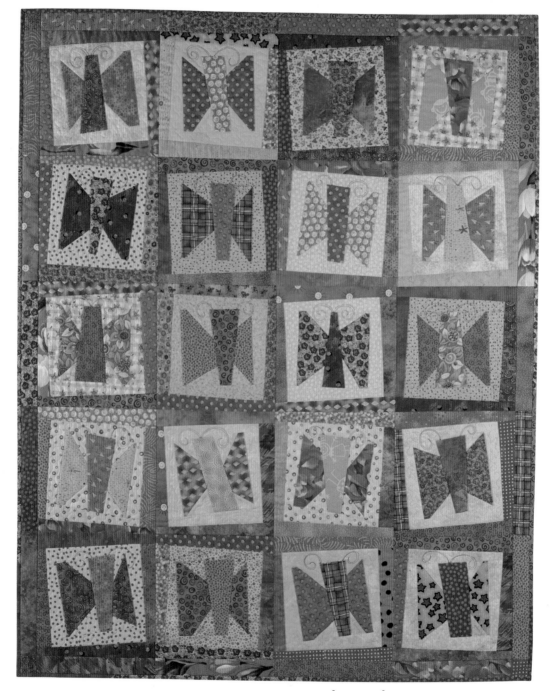

Beggar Block Butterfliez #2- Springtime by Jan Mullen, 43^1/$_2$" x 53^1/$_2$", 2000.

THE ORIGINAL BEGGAR BLOCK

UNITS/TECHNIQUES USED

Three-Patchez units

and Melon Patchez units, two corners covered,

combine to make Beggar Block Butterfliez blocks.

Refer to the cutting and piecing instructions for the Three-Patchez unit on page 16, and for the Melon Patchez unit on page 35.

I chose to use the Melon Patchez recipe rather than the Single Flying Goosez recipe because I felt the corners needed only sparse coverage.

COLOR STORY

These could have just as easily been brown moths, but why not pretty, cheerful butterflies? I chose to use happy, strong springtime colors bouncing off shining yellows. A bright array of colors included lots of that beautiful blue of fine weather skies.

Quilt Size: 43½" x 53½"

Block Size and Set: Blocks are 6" square, set four by five for a total of twenty blocks. With the addition of borders the blocks are 10" finished.

FABRIC REQUIREMENTS

Butterflies = 1 yard of assorted colors

Backgrounds = 2 yards of assorted yellows

Block Borders = 1½ yards of assorted colors

Outer Borders = ½ yard of assorted colors

CUTTING & PIECING THE QUILT BODY

Beggar Block Butterfliez Blocks

Pair up twenty butterflies fabrics to make ten happy pairs.

Cut the ten pairs of 6½" x 7½" rectangles from these butterflies fabrics. (I cut eleven sets and only used the best twenty blocks in the quilt.)

Slice, then switch the middle sections as if you were piecing Three-Patchez units, Steps 1, 2, and 3 as shown on page 16.

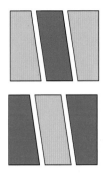

Switching the pieces

Cut forty 4"-ish squares from background fabrics. You will need two squares per block. Slice these in half-ish from corner to corner.

Follow the instructions for piecing a Melon Patchez unit, Steps 1 to 5 on page 35, but cover only the two inner corners of the outer Three-Patchez sections.

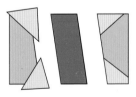

Covering the inner corners

Stitch the sections together as for piecing Three-Patchez units, Steps 4 and 5.

Backgrounds for Each Block

Cut two strips 2" x 6½" for the side backgrounds.

Cut two strips 2" x 9½" for the top and bottom backgrounds. Sew these on and then trim the block back to a skewed 8½" square as shown on page 10. Skew some right and some left.

Borders for Each Block

Sides: Cut two strips 2" x 8½".

Top and bottom: Cut two strips 2" x 11½". Add these to the block, and then trim the block to a skewed 10½" square as shown on page 10. Skew some right and some left.

OUTER BORDERS

Cut twenty strips 2" x 10½".

Cut four 2" squares for corners.

Sides: Piece together five border strips for each side. Sew to the quilt body.

Top and the bottom: Piece together four border strips for each border. Add a corner square onto each end. Sew to the quilt body.

MACHINE QUILTING

Detail of Beggar Block
Butterfliez #2-Springtime

I felt only the backgrounds needed quilting, and they were treated to wavy lines with curly ends that somehow reminded me of fluttering wings and butterflies' flight. In a strong contrasting thread I just had to quilt antennae on their head. This was double stitched and merely filled in the space available. I think it would also look lovely hand quilted in a bold running stitch and with button eyes. Next time!

Making Pinwheelz Like Mine

Pinwheelz by Jan Mullen, 42¹/₂" x 54¹/₂", 2000.

THE ORIGINAL PINWHEELS BLOCK

UNITS/TECHNIQUES USED

Cross-Patchez units

and Cover Corner Trianglez units

combine to make Pinwheelz blocks.

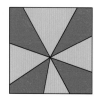

The new and improved Pinwheelz block

I chose to use the Cross-Patchez recipe rather than the Four-Patchez recipe so I could slice at strong angles, but I could have added the "extra crooked cutting allowance" to the Four-Patchez recipe and the results would have been exactly the same.

Cover Corner Trianglez units are used for the outer border.

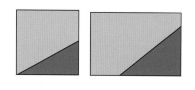

Unit 1   *Unit 2*

Refer to the cutting and piecing instructions for the Cross-Patchez unit on page 21, and for the Cover Corner Trianglez unit on page 34.

I added the "extra crooked cutting allowance" on the triangles, as well, to make it easier to cover the larger pieces of the backgrounds. The measurement I took as the background square in Step 3 was half the length of the finished block, or about 3"-ish.

COLOR STORY

With this quilt I felt it was time to break out the purples for the background because I've never made a full-blown purple quilt before. The usual brights bounce off the backgrounds. Purple tends to bring out a strong response in everyone—you'll either love this one or hate it.

Quilt Size: 42½" x 54½"

Block Size and Set: Blocks are 6" square, set six by eight for a total of forty-eight blocks.

FABRIC REQUIREMENTS

Backgrounds = 2½ yards of assorted purples

Pinwheels = 2 yards of assorted bright colors

Inner Borders = ¼ yard of dark purple

Outer Borders = 1 yard of mixed bright colors

CUTTING & PIECING THE QUILT BODY

Exploded pinwheel block

Cut forty-eight 8"-ish squares from background fabrics.

Slice according to piecing Cross-Patchez, Step 2, page 21. We aren't stacking and switching here. Slice some backgrounds and skew some left and some right.

Cut forty-eight pairs of 5"-ish squares from pinwheels fabrics. Cut them in half-ish from corner to corner.

Cover the corners of all the Cross-Patchez pieces following the piecing instructions for Cover Corner Trianglez, Steps 1 to 4, page 34.

For the best pinwheel effect I try to:

1. Make sure the pinwheel fabrics meet happily in the centers.

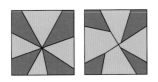

Happy and unhappy meetings

2. Choose the corners to be covered so the pinwheels fabric covers the four outer corners of the block. If the background fabrics cover the corners the block will look more like a cross.

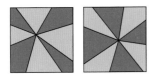

The pinwheel and the cross

Remember that the outer edge corners do not have to be perfectly covered as you will trim the units to block size later.

Piece the units together following Steps 4 to 6 of Cross-Patchez, trimming the blocks back to $6\frac{1}{2}$" square.

Arrange and sew the blocks together to form the quilt body.

INNER BORDERS

Sides: Cut two strips $1\frac{1}{2}$" x $48\frac{1}{2}$". Add to the quilt body.

Top and bottom: Cut two strips $1\frac{1}{2}$" x $38\frac{1}{2}$". Add to the quilt body.

OUTER BORDERS

The border is made up of two different sizes of Cover Corner Trianglez.

Unit 1 (80 needed)

Cut eighty $2\frac{1}{2}$" squares from assorted brights.

Cut forty $3\frac{1}{2}$"-ish squares from brights also. Cut them in half-ish from corner to corner.

Piece these units as Cover Corner Trianglez.

Unit 2 (8 needed)

Cut eight $2\frac{1}{2}$" x $3\frac{1}{2}$" rectangles from assorted brights.

Cut four $3\frac{1}{2}$"-ish squares from the brights. Cut them in half-ish from corner to corner.

Piece these units as the Cover Corner Trianglez.

For the sides, piece twenty-two of Unit 1 together in random directions. Add a Unit 2 to each end. Sew to the quilt body.

For the top and bottom, piece sixteen of Unit 1 together in random directions. Add a Unit 2 to each end, then finish the ends with another Unit 1. Sew to the quilt body.

MACHINE QUILTING

Detail of Pinwheelz

The purple backgrounds are simply held with double-stitched curls that radiate out from the centers. Wind patterns perhaps?

 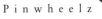

Making Milky Wayz Like Mine

Milky Wayz by Jan Mullen, 48¹/₂" x 58¹/₂", 2000.

THE ORIGINAL MILKY WAY BLOCK

UNITS/TECHNIQUES USED

Nine-Patchez units

and Cover Corner Trianglez units

combine to make Milky Wayz blocks.

These are bordered by more Cover Corner Trianglez units.

Refer to the cutting and piecing instructions for the Nine-Patchez units on page 19, and for the Cover Corner Trianglez unit on page 34.

For the Nine-Patchez, I chose to use only one fabric for the backgrounds instead of stacking and switching. I changed the centers to a different fabric with the "using a cut piece as a template method" on page 23.

After the blocks are made, their four corners are then covered to continue the whirling effect.

COLOR STORY

While playing one day I paired one of my seldom-used orange fabrics with a teally, not-very-bright green fabric, and loved the effect! This combination was waiting in the wings for the right quilt. Here it is. Calming bluey greens and greeny blues teamed with oranges, up-scaled to reds, and down-scaled to yellows. The hot pink border that moves toward violet was an unusual choice, but I love it.

Quilt Size: 48½" x 58½"

Block Size and Set: Blocks are 10" square set four by five for a total of twenty blocks.

FABRIC REQUIREMENTS

Blocks/Border Backgrounds = 3¼ yards of assorted blue/greens

Blocks/Border Stars = 2¼ yards of assorted oranges, reds, and yellows

Inner Border = ⅓ yard of assorted hot pinks

CUTTING & PIECING THE QUILT BODY

Cut twenty 11½" squares from background fabrics.

Slice according to piecing Nine-Patchez, Step 2 on page 20.

Replace the center squares with stars fabrics using the template method described on page 23.

Cut twenty sets of two 4½"-ish squares from stars fabric to match the ones chosen for each center square. Cut these in half-ish from corner to corner.

Cover the four middle sides background pieces with these following the piecing instructions for Cover Corner Trianglez, Steps 1 to 4, on page 34. Make sure that the triangles all point either clockwise or counter-clockwise on each block.

Sew the pieces and units together following the piecing instructions for Nine-Patchez, Steps 4 and 5 on page 20.

Arrange the blocks in a pleasing order. Number them so they may be easily placed back in this order.

Cut twenty sets of two 5"-ish squares from stars fabrics. Cut these in half-ish from corner to corner.

Place these triangles at the intersections of each block. Where four corners meet use a set of four triangles. Where two corners meet use a pair of triangles. On the last four corners use the last two pairs.

Sew on these triangles, following the piecing for Cover Corner Trianglez, Steps 1 to 4. Make sure the sets or pairs turn either clockwise or counter-clockwise.

Sew the blocks together to form the quilt body.

INNER BORDERS

Sides: Piece and cut two strips 1¹/₂" x 50¹/₂". Add to the quilt body.

Top and bottom: Piece and cut two strips 1¹/₂" x 42¹/₂". Add to the quilt body.

OUTER BORDERS

The border is made up of three different units.

Unit 1 (10 needed)

Cut ten 3¹/₂" x 10¹/₂" rectangles from background fabrics.

Unit 2 (8 needed)

Cut eight 3¹/₂" x 11¹/₂" rectangles from background fabrics.

Unit 3 (4 needed)

Cut four 3¹/₂" squares from background fabrics.

Before you begin sewing, lay out the border units around the quilt body in the following order.

Sides: For each side place three Unit 1 rectangles with a Unit 2 rectangle on each end.

Top and bottom: Place two Unit 1 rectangles with a Unit 2 on each end; add a Unit 3 square on each end.

Cut twenty 5"-ish squares from stars fabric to match and complete each half and quarter star started in the quilt body. Cut them in half-ish from corner to corner.

Place and sew the triangles according to the photo of the quilt using the Cover Corner Trianglez piecing instructions on page 34.

Piece two side borders together, then the two top and bottom border units together. Sew these borders to the quilt body.

MACHINE QUILTING

Detail of Milky Wayz

The backgrounds of the blocks required filling, as well as suggested movement. I quilted curly-tailed lines in a circular pattern, changing direction from block to block. The borders continued with a directional breezy pattern, three double-stitched wavy lines per border unit, to enclose the turning stars.

Making Churn Dashez Like Mine

Churn Dashez # 4-Firing the Flamez by Jan Mullen, 50½" x 58½", 2000.

THE ORIGINAL CHURN DASH BLOCK

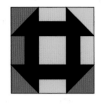

UNITS/TECHNIQUES USED

Nine-Patchez units

Cover Corner Trianglez units

and Cover Corner Rectanglez units

combine to make Churn Dashez blocks.

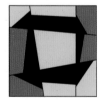

Refer to the cutting and piecing instructions for the Nine-Patchez units on page 20, for the Cover Corner Trianglez unit on page 34, and for the Cover Corner Rectanglez unit on page 41.

For the Cover Corner Rectanglez I chose to work from strips rather than working out individual measurements, but I still used the recipe.

I estimated that the relevant pieces would be roughly one-third of the cut block size, which is 3½". For the length I added an inch per piece—18" for each of the four pieces plus a bit for exaggeration—20". For the width, I started with the same 3½", and halved it to 1¾". Then I added the required extra inch, which brought it to 2¾"; this time I decided to round the measurement down to 2½"-ish as I like these pieces looking leaner.

COLOR STORY

Where did this devilish combination hail from? Strong blacks and some equally forceful whites provided a starting point. The reds seemed to be a great counterpoint to the blacks and whites—but how did the yellow fit in? My inability to stop at two colors made me shove in those flickering lights to make it glow. Perhaps most suitable for a teenage boy!

Quilt Size: 50½" x 58½"

Block Size and Set: Blocks are 8" square, set five by six for a total of thirty blocks.

FABRIC REQUIREMENTS

Blocks/Borders Backgrounds = 4½ yards of assorted reds and yellows

Blocks/Borders Focus Fabrics = 4½ yards of assorted blacks and whites

Inner Border = ¼ yard of a black print

CUTTING & PIECING THE QUILT BODY

Cut forty-eight 9½" squares from background fabrics. Place them in groups of four, five, or six to achieve the mixed background effect.

Slice, following the piecing instructions for Nine-Patchez, Steps 1 to 3, on page 20, but randomly switch pieces among the group.

Focus Fabrics

For each background square: Cut two 4½"-ish squares. Cut these in half-ish from corner to corner.

Cut a 2½" x 20"-ish strip. Cut this to size, as needed, for the Cover Corner Rectanglez.

For each block: Cover the four corner pieces of backgrounds following the piecing for Cover Corner Trianglez, Steps 1 to 4.

Cover the four side pieces following the piecing for Cover Corner Rectanglez, Steps 1 to 5.

Sew the units into blocks following the piecing for Nine-Patchez, Steps 4 and 5.

Arrange the blocks and sew together to form the quilt body.

INNER BORDERS

Sides: Piece and cut two strips 1½" x 48½". Sew to the quilt body.

Top and bottom: Cut two strips 1½" x 42½". Sew to the quilt body.

OUTER BORDERS

The outer borders are made up of Churn Dashez blocks that are two different sizes: Block 1 is 4" square finished, and Block 2 is 4" x 4½" finished.

Block 1 (32 needed)

Cut thirty-two 5½" squares from background fabrics.

For Each Background: Cut two 2½"-ish squares from focus fabrics. Cut these in half-ish from corner to corner.

Cut a strip 2" x 10"-ish from focus fabrics. Trim the strip as needed.

Block 2 (16 needed)

Cut sixteen 5½" x 6" rectangles from background fabrics.

For Each Background: Cut two 2½"-ish squares from focus fabrics. Cut these in half-ish from corner to corner.

Cut a 2" x 11"-ish strip from focus fabrics. Cut this to size as you need it.

Piece all the blocks as you did for the quilt body blocks.

Sides: Sew together two sets: eight of Block 1 with two Block 2's added to each end. Add to the quilt body.

Top and bottom: Sew together two sets: six of Block 1 with two Block 2's added to each end, then finish the ends with another Block 1. Sew to the quilt body.

MACHINE QUILTING

Detail of Churn Dashez #4—Firing the Flamez

Following the fiery theme, double-stitched wavy lines and curls wafted in and around the blocks, both big and small.

Making Devilz Clawz Like Mine

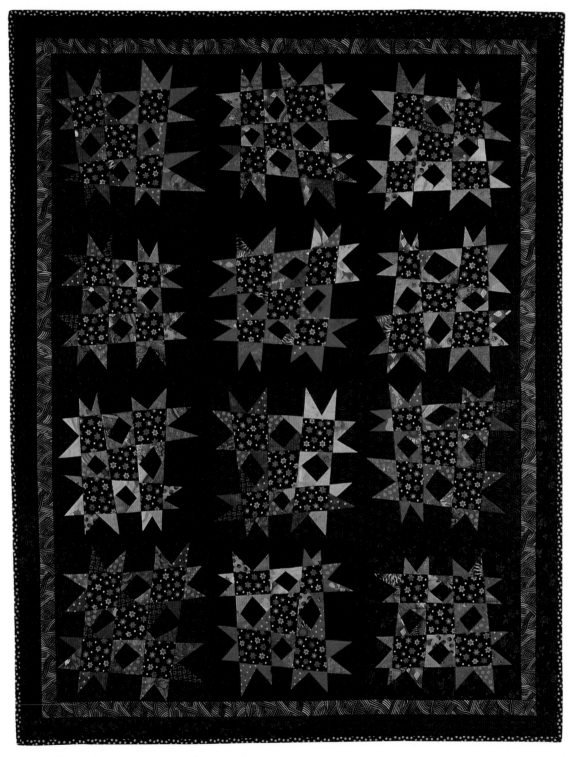

Devilz Clawz by Jan Mullen, 35¹/₂" x 45¹/₂", 2000.

THE ORIGINAL DEVILS CLAWS BLOCK

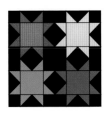

UNITS/TECHNIQUES USED

Twenty Five-Patchez (an extension of the Nine-Patchez unit)

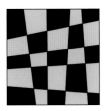

Single Flying Goosez units

and Melon Patchez units

combine to make Devilz Clawz blocks.

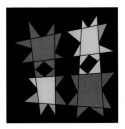

Refer to the cutting and piecing instructions for the Nine-Patchez units on page 20, for the Single Flying Goosez unit on page 36, and for the Melon Patchez unit on page 35.

For ease, I applied the Single Flying Goosez recipe for determining the size of the triangles, then used the same size triangle for the Melon Patchez units. I cut some bigger to create some longer claws.

COLOR STORY

A lovely fat quarter of fabric decided a lot about this quilt. The black fabric with colored stars on it helped determine the color scheme, the number of blocks made, and, as a result, the small size of the quilt. I would have loved to make it bigger and could have substituted another fabric as I usually would, but I felt this time the uniformity of the feature centers helped to make the colored claws sparkle. In most blocks I had one color blending into another. The border was the trickiest decision, and in the end I chose a fabric with all the colors of the quilt in it.

Next time I'd go for a luminous blue, or a stunning aqua, or a vibrant green . . . next time . . .

Quilt Size: 35$\frac{1}{2}$" x 45$\frac{1}{2}$"

Block Size and Set: Blocks are 10" square, set three by four for a total of twelve blocks.

FABRIC REQUIREMENTS

Backgrounds/Outer Border = 1$\frac{3}{4}$ yards of assorted blacks

Pads = $\frac{1}{2}$ yard of a strong (bold/busy) print

Claws = 1 yard of assorted colors

Inner Border = $\frac{1}{4}$ yard of a colorful/dramatic print

CUTTING & PIECING THE QUILT BODY

Cut twelve 12$\frac{1}{2}$" squares from background fabrics.

Slice each square four times, in both directions, as you would do for Twenty-Five-Patchez.

Change the five feature pieces from background fabric to pads fabric with the "using a cut piece as a template" method on page 23.

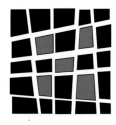

Replacing some pieces

Working on each block individually may help keep order here:

Cut sixteen 2"-ish squares from claws fabrics. Slice these in half-ish from corner to corner.

Following the piecing instructions for Single Flying Goosez and

Melon Patchez on pages 35 and 36, cover the corners of the pieces shown. Make sure they return to their correct position.

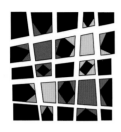

*Flying Goosez and
Melon Patchez complete*

Sew the pieces and units back together as you would for Nine-Patchez, Steps 4 and 5.

Arrange the completed blocks and sew together to form the quilt body.

INNER BORDERS

Sides: Cut two strips $1\frac{1}{2}$" x $40\frac{1}{2}$". Sew to the quilt body.

Top and bottom: Cut two strips $1\frac{1}{2}$" x $32\frac{1}{2}$". Sew to the quilt body.

OUTER BORDERS

Sides: Piece and cut two strips 2" x $42\frac{1}{2}$". Sew to the quilt body.

Top and bottom: Cut two strips 2" x $35\frac{1}{2}$". Sew to the quilt body.

MACHINE QUILTING

Detail of Devilz Clawz

From experience I know that my style of quilting doesn't show up very well on black fabrics—luckily the detail of the blocks and colors didn't need fancy work, so stars and spirals filled the backgrounds amply. Lines with curls worked their way around the black border. Simple!

Making Snailz Trailz Like Mine

Snailz Trailz by Jan Mullen, 46¹/₂" x 55¹/₂", 2000.

THE ORIGINAL SNAIL TRAIL BLOCK

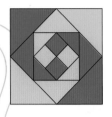

UNITS/TECHNIQUES USED

Four-Patchez units

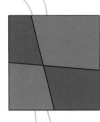

and Triple Squarez-in-Squarez units

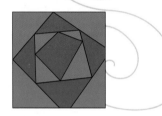

combine to make a Snailz Trailz block.

Refer to the cutting and piecing instructions for the Four-Patchez units on page 17, and for the Triple Squarez-in-Squarez unit on page 59.

To find the finished size of the Four-Patchez unit to be placed in the center of the Triple Squarez-in-Squarez unit, I followed the cutting recipe on page 59, Steps 1 to 3. This helped me determine the center square measurement of 3½" square, and I added the usual seam allowance to make it 4" square, then added the Four-Patchez trimming allowance for a final size of 4½"-ish square. I cut two squares this size, then stacked, sliced, switched, and sewed them to make two center squares.

COLOR STORY

Sweet and happy brights were a definite theme here. Pleasant pinks, yapping yellows, bouncy blues, glowing greens, and pretty purples were combined in many different pairings. I set these almost randomly, trying to achieve a nice even mix of colors rather than working at the strong graphic possibilities this block offers.

Quilt Size: 46½" x 55½"

Block Size and Set: Blocks are 9" square, set four by five for a total of twenty blocks.

FABRIC REQUIREMENTS

Blocks = 4 yards of assorted brights; for example, 2 yards of light and 2 yards of dark to make the pattern work

Inner Border = ¼ yard of purple stripe

Outer Border = 2 yards of assorted brights

CUTTING & PIECING THE QUILT BODY

Cut twenty 4½"-ish squares from block fabrics. Pair them up and make them up as Four-Patchez units, Steps 1 to 5. You can relax here and match the center points, not the edges.

When they are made up they must be trimmed slightly to make them crooked.

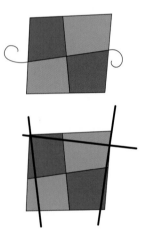

Rough Four-Patchez trimmed to shape

Now, matching the fabrics to each block as you go, sew on each of the three rounds, working the colors in a clockwise direction. Follow the piecing instructions for Triple Squarez-in-Squarez, Steps 2 to 6, page 60.

Round 1

Cut forty 4"-ish squares, two per block, from block fabrics. Cut these in half-ish from corner to corner.

Round 2

Cut forty 5½"-ish squares, two per block, from block fabrics. Cut these in half-ish from corner to corner.

Round 3

Cut forty 7"-ish squares, two per block, from block fabrics. Cut these in half-ish from corner to corner.

Trim the blocks to 9½" square.

Arrange them and piece together to form the quilt body.

INNER BORDERS

Sides: Piece and cut two strips 1½" x 45½". Sew to the quilt body.

Top and bottom: Cut two strips 1½" x 38½". Sew to the quilt body.

OUTER BORDERS

The borders are made from Four-Patchez pushed to a diamond shape by adding triangles to each side and then trimming.

Cut forty 4"-ish squares from border fabrics. Pair them up and make them up as Four-Patchez units, Steps 1 to 5. You can relax and match the points at the centers, not the edges. When they are made up they must be trimmed to make them crooked.

Cut eighty 4"-ish squares; two are needed per unit from border fabrics. Cut these in half-ish from corner to corner. Add to each side of the Four-Patchez units.

Trim these down to three different sizes:

Unit 1 = 4½" x 5", twenty needed.

Unit 2 = 4½" x 5½", sixteen needed.

Unit 3 = 4½" square, four needed.

Sides: For each side border, sew two sets each: six of Unit 1 rectangles with two Unit 2 rectangles sewn to each end.

Top and bottom: For each border, sew together four Unit 1 rectangles to two Unit 2 rectangles and add a Unit 3 square to each end.

Sew the borders to the quilt body.

MACHINE QUILTING

Detail of Snailz Trailz

Curls make their final appearance here: pairs of the long, leggy variety starting the journey with a star, heart, spot, hook or clover leaf in the middle, before moving off as double-stitched lines, separating and veering off to fill background space with their spiral tails. They make their way out from the center in all four directions.

CHAPTER 8

Settings and Such

As we approach the end of the path, I couldn't leave you without passing on a few ideas about settings for the blocks and units you have made.

I have been very lucky to have a small group of enthusiastic students who have been willing guinea pigs, patiently working through these chapters just half a step behind me. Some of them started out with strong ideas about what they wanted to achieve; others have let the blocks decide the way their top was to be finished. This chapter is illustrated with some of the quilts and quilt tops they have completed.

If you follow my suggestion of working through Chapters 3 to 6, making sample units along the way, you will have enough units to make a sampler quilt. You may choose to place the blocks randomly, just working on the balance of color, line, and pattern, adding extra blocks when needed to bring the top up to size. Marilyn Dillon chose to go this way, working on mixing the colors and textures to end up with something different from her usual style. We loved her 6" Churn Dashez so much we pleaded with her to use these as her fillers.

Sampler by Marilyn Dillon, 49" x 62", Perth, Western Australia, 2000.

You may choose to make a medallion quilt, working out from the center and adding on round after round. Julie Howell's quilt was designed before she started any cutting; she made her large number of blocks "to order." With very few changes or additions, but lots of time spent arranging and fine tuning, she has a stunning quilt. In some rounds there is a variety of blocks, and in others definition is maintained and the variety of previous rows contained by some strong repeats of single blocks.

Medallion Sampler by Julie Howell, 79" square, Perth, Western Australia, 2000.

Debra McHolick worked a different way. After every class she would make up blocks to suit what she had put together the previous week. If you look closely, you can see that she started with rectangles, surrounded them with triangles, leaving logs and curves to have double billing in the final round.

Sampler Quilt by Debra J. McHolick, 47½" x 56", Perth, Western Australia, 2000.

You may choose to place all of your large blocks in the center, building them up to a uniform size with borders. Jan Holland made her Grannie'z Fanz float by bordering them in the same block background fabrics. Her outer border is a selection of small blocks.

St. Clements by Jan Holland, 50" x 62", Perth, Western Australia, 2000.

In similar style Tess Marks chose to combine various sized sample blocks in the quilt body, then border this with smaller blocks. Here she combined different sizes by building up rectangles, then rows, and sewing the rows together. This is a favorite block disguise of mine, and it helps if you are good at jigsaw puzzles!

Hot Spotz by Tess Marks, 56"x 57", Perth, Western Australia, 2000.

You may like to make a quilt with two blocks. Sometimes alternating blocks creates another secondary pattern or, as shown here, the second block can be a frame. Tess Marks has given us two versions: the first has Beggar Block Butterfliez surrounded by Pinwheelz, the second has Snailz Trailz bordered by Double Squarez-in-Squarez. Both are full of color and interest, both are wonderful pairings.

Mothz and Pinwheelz by Tess Marks, 48½"x 48½", Perth, Western Australia, 2000.

Hot Chilli Salsa by Tess Marks, 34½"x 34½",
Perth, Western Australia, 2000.

You may work with one block only, but make it up in different sizes. Debra McHolick has taken a galaxy full of blunt Sawtooth Starz in various sizes and created a top that is pure quirky, "pointless" delight.

Well, that's it for now, our path together stops here. I'm leaving you to decide which fork you take. Will you integrate these easy techniques into the occasional quilt, or will you be fully converted and continue to journey forward in this free manner?

Whichever way you go—enjoy cutting loose!

Under The Southern Cross by Debra J. McHolick, 42"x 56", Perth, Western Australia, 2000.

ABOUT THE AUTHOR

Australian quiltmaker extraordinaire Jan Mullen trained as a secondary art/craft teacher majoring in textiles before meeting the first love of her life, Ben. Together they set about producing three major works, their darlings—Brodie, Keelan, and Miffany. Rather than continuing to work in this theme, her second love, textiles, re-emerged and started to dominate their lives. First quilts were made for family members, then an opportunity to teach quiltmaking locally followed. Finally, a commercial venture was consolidated with the start of Stargazey Quilts in 1996.

Only a few years down the track, Stargazey Quilts has published an extensive catalog of original, crooked patterns. In designing fabrics for Marcus Brothers, new challenges continually appear that introduce Jan to other related disciplines. She does enjoy teaching others her wicked ways, particularly when guiding students toward working more confidently and intuitively with color. She also enjoys showing them that it is often possible to dispense with rules. In rare moments she likes to produce art quilts, walk the beach with Celeste and Rocket, and fill the bikkie jar for the darlings.

Jan can be contacted at:

Stargazey Quilts; 9-100 Stirling Highway, North Fremantle, Western Australia, 6159
ph + 61 8 9433 3129
fax + 61 8 9433 3109

email; jan@stargazey.com
web site: www.stargazey.com

Stargazey Quilts patterns are distributed in North America by Quilters' Resource, 2211 N. Elston Avenue, Chicago, IL 60614.
(713) 278-5695   Fax (773) 278-1348

Index

Other Fine Books From C&T Publishing:

Along the Garden Path: More Quilters and Their Gardens, Jean Wells and Valori Wells

An Amish Adventure: 2nd Edition, Roberta Horton

Appliqué 12 Easy Ways! Charming Quilts, Giftable Projects & Timeless Techniques, Elly Sienkiewicz

Art & Inspirations: Ruth B. McDowell, Ruth B. McDowell

The Art of Machine Piecing: Quality Workmanship Through a Colorful Journey, Sally Collins

The Art of Classic Quiltmaking, Harriet Hargrave and Sharyn Craig

Block Magic: Over 50 Fun & Easy Blocks Made From Squares and Rectangles, Nancy Johnson-Srebro

Civil War Women: Their Quilts, Their Roles, and Activities for Re-Enactors, Barbara Brackman

Color From the Heart: Seven Great Ways to Make Quilts with Colors You Love, Gai Perry

Color Play: Easy Steps to Imaginative Color in Quilts, Joen Wolfrom

Cotton Candy Quilts: Using Feedsacks, Vintage and Reproduction Fabrics, Mary Mashuta

Curves in Motion: Quilt Designs & Techniques, Judy B. Dales

Diane Phalen Quilts: 10 Projects to Celebrate the Seasons, Diane Phalen

Easy Pieces: Creative Color Play with Two Simple Blocks, Margaret Miller

Everything Flowers: Quilts from the Garden, Jean and Valori Wells

Exploring Machine Trapunto: New Dimensions, Hari Walner

Fabric Shopping with Alex Anderson, Seven Projects to Help You: Make Successful Choices, Build Your Confidence, Add to Your Fabric Stash, Alex Anderson

Fantastic Fabric Folding: Innovative Quilting Projects, Rebecca Wat

Flower Pounding: Quilt Projects for All Ages, Amy Sandrin & Ann Frischkorn

Freddy's House: Brilliant Color in Quilts, Freddy Moran

Free Stuff for Crafty Kids on the Internet, Judy Heim and Gloria Hansen

Free Stuff for Pet Lovers on the Internet, Gloria Hansen

Free Stuff for Quilters on the Internet, 2nd Ed., Judy Heim and Gloria Hansen

Free Stuff for Sewing Fanatics on the Internet, Judy Heim and Gloria Hansen

Free Stuff for Stitchers on the Internet, Judy Heim and Gloria Hansen

Free Stuff for Traveling Quilters on the Internet, Gloria Hansen

Free-Style Quilts: A "No Rules" Approach, Susan Carlson

Ghost Layers & Color Washes: Three Steps to Spectacular Quilts, Katie Pasquini Masopust

Hand Appliqué with Alex Anderson: Seven Projects for Hand Appliqué, Alex Anderson

Hand Quilting with Alex Anderson: Six Projects for Hand Quilters, Alex Anderson

Heirloom Machine Quilting, Third Edition, Harriet Hargrave

Impressionist Palette, Gai Perry

Impressionist Quilts, Gai Perry

In the Nursery: Creative Quilts and Designer Touches, Jennifer Sampou & Carolyn Schmitz

Kaleidoscopes: Wonders of Wonder, Cozy Baker

Kaleidoscopes & Quilts, Paula Nadelstern

Make Any Block Any Size, Joen Wolfrom

Mastering Machine Appliqué, Harriet Hargrave

Mastering Quilt Marking: Marking Tools & Techniques, Choosing Stencils, Matching Borders & Corners, Pepper Cory

The New Sampler Quilt, Diana Leone

On the Surface: Thread Embellishment & Fabric Manipulation, Wendy Hill

Patchwork Persuasion: Fascinating Quilts from Traditional Designs, Joen Wolfrom

The Photo Transfer Handbook: Snap It, Print It, Stitch It!, Jean Ray Laury

Pieced Flowers, Ruth B. McDowell

Piecing: Expanding the Basics, Ruth B. McDowell

Plaids & Stripes: The Use of Directional Fabrics in Quilts, Roberta Horton

Quilt It for Kids: 11 Projects, Sports, Fantasy & Animal Themes, Quilts for Children of All Ages, Pam Bono

The Quilted Garden: Design & Make Nature-Inspired Quilts, Jane A. Sassaman

Quilting with the Muppets: The Jim Henson Company in Association with Sesame Workshop

Quilts, Quilts, and More Quilts! Diana McClun and Laura Nownes

Rotary Cutting with Alex Anderson: Tips, Techniques, and Projects, Alex Anderson

Rx for Quilters: Stitcher-Friendly Advice for Every Body, Susan Delaney Mech, M.D.

Say It with Quilts: Diana McClun and Laura Nownes

Setting Solutions, Sharyn Craig

Shadow Redwork™ with Alex Anderson: 24 Designs to Mix and Match, Alex Anderson

Smashing Sets: Exciting Ways to Arrange Quilt Blocks, Margaret J. Miller

Snowflakes & Quilts, Paula Nadelstern

Special Delivery Quilts, Patrick Lose

Start Quilting with Alex Anderson: Six Projects for First-Time Quilters, Alex Anderson

Stitch 'n Flip Quilts: 14 Fantastic Projects, Valori Wells

Stripes in Quilts, Mary Mashuta

A Thimbleberries Housewarming: 22 Projects for Quilters, Lynette Jensen

Through the Garden Gate: Quilters and Their Gardens, Jean and Valori Wells

Travels with Peaky and Spike: Doreen Speckmann's Quilting Adventures, Doreen Speckmann

Wild Birds: Designs for Appliqué & Quilting, Carol Armstrong

Wildflowers: Designs for Appliqué & Quilting, Carol Armstrong

Willowood: Further Adventures in Buttonhole Stitch Appliqué, Jean Wells

For more information write for a free catalog:
C&T Publishing, Inc.
P.O. Box 1456
Lafayette, CA 94549
(800) 284-1114
e-mail: ctinfo@ctpub.com
website: www.ctpub.com

For quilting supplies:
Cotton Patch Mail Order
3405 Hall Lane, Dept. CTB
Lafayette, CA 94549
(800) 835-4418
(925) 283-7883
e-mail: quiltusa@yahoo.com
website: www.quiltusa.com